Going Green Together

How to Align Employees with Green Strategies

By Frank Röttgers

ISBN: 978-3-00-032898-5

Library of Congress Control Number: 2010916613

Edition 1

ACKNOWLEDGEMENTS

My thanks go to James Curran for organising the interviews, and my brother Dirk for always being at hand with help and advice. I am also grateful to the strategic management lunch council for all its support and would like to thank Brian Gallagher and Trevor Woodhouse in particular for their contributions.

TABLE OF CONTENTS

ABSTRACT

At a time when 'going green' is at the top of the agenda of many organisations one of the most critical success factors of strategy implementation escapes the notice of many theorists and practitioners. As employees are considered the linchpin of organisations' strategic operational success, the objective of this thesis is to determine the impact of employee strategic alignment on green strategy implementation. Moreover, this thesis aims at providing theorists and practitioners with insights into how to align employees with green strategies to facilitate a flawless realisation of organisations' environmental goals. Comparing the gained primary data to the existing literature allows the development of an empirically and theoretically grounded argument stating that employee strategic alignment is vital for a successful green strategy implementation. Despite the finding that organisations with an environmental focus have the advantage that a large number of employees automatically commit to their green strategies due to personal identification with the underlying goals, their endeavours to align the remaining employees is crucial to the overall success of the strategy. By cultivating a green framework, organisations are able to increase the amount of strategically aligned employees, embed green thinking in daily routines, and induce a more action-related behaviour towards the implementation of a green strategy. To deliver the essential cornerstones for this framework, practitioners need to create an open and forgiving company culture, extensively communicate their intentions, unveil a proactive leadership style, and offer the right incentives. Thereby, organisations determine the make or break of their environmental objectives and lay the foundation for a sustainable competitive advantage.

CHAPTER ONE

INTRODUCTION

1.1 Background

'Going green' has evolved into a common catchphrase across today's business landscape while strategic managers discuss best practices for formulating and implementing green strategies vigorously as never before (Sturdivant 2008). The reasons for the topicality of companies going green and the ongoing discussions about the right way to approach it are manifold. Whereas some organisations go green in order to be compliant with governmental regulations or feel responsible towards the continued existence of the planet and their corporate social responsibility activities, other organisations go green in order to decrease cost, increase their profitability, and thereby gain a competitive advantage (Nidumolu et al. 2009; Wilson 2008). Two widely known facts, which receive much attention in today's business world, lie behind this green wave: the limits of the natural world and the growing concern of stakeholders about the environment (Esty and Winston 2009). While issues such as global warming, resource constraints, loss of biodiversity, and water scarcity constrain business operations, threaten the planet's well-being, and lead to a realignment of markets, a vast majority of stakeholders insists that organisations pay attention to these issues.

Especially governments, customers, and employees do not longer turn a blind eye on environmental unfriendly business practices and call for action when it comes to turning organisations' operations green (Esty and Winston 2009). Organisations that ignore these aspects neglect the fact that a growing green economy is emerging in the first decade of the twenty-first century. This new decade addresses the world's environmental challenges while creating new opportunities for those companies that outperform the wasteful and polluting production and business processes of their competition by implementing environmentally friendly and cleaner business models and strategies (Makower 2008). Indeed, almost every Fortune 500 company today has recognised the demand for green strategies not just as a defence mechanism to retain legitimacy and the right to operate, but as core of their mission and reason for being (Marcus and Fremeth 2009). Realising that the creation of business value and improvements in operations and reputation are often related to the staff's alignment with the organisation's green strategy and everyone's involvement in the organisation's mission, employees play a major role in the emerging green economy of this century.

1.2 Purpose and Nature of the Research Project

Strategies for going green and the role of employees in implementing those strategies have become a relevant area of academic research and in day-to-day business life (Kotler and Lee 2005; Esty and Winston 2009). However, while many authors and practitioners write about and concern themselves with why and how to formulate green strategies, very little research exists on how a successful implementation of a green strategy can be attained and what impact employees have on putting a theoretically formulated strategy into practice. The purpose and nature of this research project is therefore of two kinds: to complement existing academic research on the one hand and to provide practitioners and professionals with new insights on the other. In more detail, this research project is of relevance to academic researchers because it complements existing research on strategies dedicated to turn organisations green by taking a closer look at the role of employees on the successful implementation of green strategies. Furthermore, it complements existing theories on knowing-doing gaps and performance

3

paradoxes within organisations. In order to do so, it considers whether the existing theory of general business strategies is also applicable to green strategies and delivers new data on employee strategic alignment with respect to green strategies by conducting primary research in one of the world's largest electricity companies.

In a marketplace where competitive differentiation is hard to gain, green strategies and an environmental advantage also become a larger decisive element for practitioners and business professionals. Today, environmental missteps might lead to corporate scandals regarding an organisation's public relations and a decrease in an organisation's value, as well as destroy entire markets. Therefore, practitioners need to add environmental thinking to their strategic toolkit in order to make use of upside opportunities in markets that are increasingly shaped by environmental factors. Those who are able to manage environmental challenges by successfully implementing green strategies with skill will build more profitable and longer lasting businesses as well as a healthier and more liveable planet (Esty and Winston 2009). This research project will support professionals and practitioners in reaching these goals by indicating what role employees, their motivation, and their strategic alignment play when turning an organisation green. Furthermore, it is pointed out where practitioners and professionals need to intervene in order to go green successfully and information is provided on how to put a theoretically formulated green strategy into practice, illustrating the differences between the implementation of green and other strategies.

1.3 Contents of the Research Project

In order to provide practitioners and business professionals with the above mentioned new insights and narrow the gap in the literature in the fields of strategy implementation and employee strategic alignment with respect to green strategies, the contents of this research project are divided into five chapters that build upon each other in order to analyse the overall research objective. Chapter one provides an introduction into the research project by outlining the background, illustrating the purpose and nature, and stating the overall research objective of this research project.

Chapter two covers the literature review, which will be drawn upon in the research analysis when investigating the research objective based on the primary research. This chapter begins by defining green strategies and critically discusses associated strategy implementation challenges, knowing-doing gaps and performance paradoxes, and the importance of employee strategic alignment to overcome strategy implementation challenges as well as the transferability of these concepts to green strategies.

Chapter three outlines the research philosophy and identifies the appropriate research methodology. After providing the rationale for the appropriate research approach, the research design which suits the underlying research objective best and builds the foundation for the research analysis is presented.

Chapter four covers the findings and analysis of this research project. In this chapter the organisation under study as well as the interview participants and the documentation used for the analysis are introduced. Data and insights from the in-depth interview transcripts with the company under study are presented and related to the issues outlined in the literature review in order to provide coherent answers to the research questions.

Based on the findings and analysis from Chapter four, Chapter five provides a final conclusion of the overall research objective. In addition to that, a number of limitations to the research are identified, managerial implications are outlined, and recommendations as well as suggestions for future research are put forward.

1.4 Overall Research Objective

The overall research objective of this research project is to determine the impact of employee strategic alignment on the implementation of green strategies to develop explanatory theory for closing knowing-doing gaps of green strategies. Specific research questions based on issues emerging from the literature will be outlined in Chapter two.

CHAPTER TWO

LITERATURE REVIEW

2.1 Introduction

In light of the research objective, the literature review identifies key issues surrounding the research objective and critically discusses existing literature relevant for the research and analysis of the impact of employee strategic alignment on the implementation of green strategies to develop explanatory theory for closing knowing-doing gaps of green strategies. In order to serve this purpose, the following paragraph first evaluates several opinions on what is understood by the term green strategy. Following that discussion, it provides a working definition for the purpose of this research project and discusses general challenges during the implementation of strategies. Having analysed these challenges, the next paragraphs review the literature on two main challenges during the implementation of strategies, which are performance paradoxes and knowing-doing gaps. Subsequently, the literature on the role of employee strategic alignment in strategy implementation is discussed, providing an appropriate definition of the term employee strategic alignment and outlining the existing theories on how this alignment can be achieved and to what extent it is limited. The focus of the literature will then return to how the main challenges during the implementation of a strategy can be tackled by achieving employee strategic alignment and illustrate current opinions on how these theories are transferable to green strategy implementation. Resulting from this literature review, a conclusion is drawn and research questions are raised which will be addressed in the course of this research project.

2.2 Green Strategy Defined

Despite the fact that a large number of authors contribute to the extensive and ongoing discussion on green strategies within current business literature, no universal definition of what a green strategy is or what its implications are exists. Since additionally green strategies are often mentioned in connection with sustainability strategies and are sometimes referred to collectively, it is important to distinguish their different meanings and clarify what is understood by a green strategy. Several authors (e.g. Esty and Winston 2009; Makower 2008; Marshall and Brown 2003; Olson 2008; Placet et al. 2005) maintain that a green strategy is one essential component of a broader sustainability strategy. While sustainability strategies focus on propelling sustainable development and its three main goals are environmental stewardship, social responsibility, and economic wealth for the organisation as well as for its stakeholders, green strategies are directed towards only one of these goals: environmental stewardship (Placet et al. 2005). However, it is noteworthy that the three goals of sustainability strategies cannot be seen in isolation but are interlinked and support each other (Placet et al. 2005). For the purpose of this research project, Olson's (2008, p.22) definition of a green strategy is applied. It states that:

> A green strategy for an enterprise – public or private, government or commercial – is one that complements the business, operations, and asset strategies that are already well understood and often well articulated by the enterprise. A green strategy fundamentally helps an enterprise make decisions that have a positive impact on the environment.

Whereas many authors devote themselves to answering questions about why and how to *formulate* green strategies, only very few researchers scrutinise how a successful *implementation* of a green strategy can be achieved and what factors mainly contribute to putting a green strategy into action. To narrow this gap in literature, the following section will outline the theory on strategy

9

implementation, focusing on the associated challenges which arise when putting formulated strategies into practice, in order to lay the foundation for the analysis of employee alignment and its impact on the implementation of green strategies.

2.3 The Challenges of Implementing Strategies

The success of an organisation depends to a large extent on the implementation of strategies (Noble and Mokwa 1999). However, Pfeffer and Sutton (1999) argue that there is a large gap between what an organisation knows and what an organisation really does. They claim that although most of the time organisations and managers know what they should do in order to perform better, they do not put their knowledge into practice nor implement their ideas (Pfeffer and Sutton 1999). In earlier years, also other authors such as Mintzberg (1978) and Nutt (1987) pointed out that implementing a strategy is not always realised in the straightforward way it was planned during the formulation of the strategy. Mintzberg (1978) maintains that this is due to dividing the strategic process into two incoherent stages: the strategy formulation and strategy implementation. This division can lead to the failure of a strategy, because the interrelation between the two processes is ignored and the learning curve neglected. This argument is also fostered by Hambrick and Cannella (1989), as they claim the implementation of a strategy must already be considered and addressed during the strategy formulation in order to find out if the strategy is feasible and to make it less prone to error.

Pfeffer and Sutton (1999) state that the challenge of implementing strategies successfully does not lie in finding the right solution to a problem and therefore does not lie in the strategy formulation. They maintain that in the world of business there are not many secrets left which could reveal how to reach optimal performance. What separates the wheat from the chaff is therefore the ability to act and to implement strategies rather than knowing them (Pfeffer and Sutton 1999). Although Cohen (1998) partly agrees with Pfeffer and Sutton (1999) that managers often know what to do but simply do not do it, he further maintains that most managers 'actually ignore or act in contradiction to either their strongest instincts or to the data available to them' (1998, p.30) and calls this phenomenon 'the performance paradox' (1998, p.30). Cohen (1998) highlights the necessity of organisations to detect and cope with such paradoxes and illustrates possible conditions that encourage the development and allow the presence of such behaviour. However, Pfeffer and Sutton (1999) deem the performance paradox as a given fact and provide eight steps how to turn knowledge into action.

Observing the same phenomenon from two different angles, both, Cohen (1998) and Pfeffer and Sutton (1999) describe ways to tackle the challenge of implementing already known strategies to solve a problem. Taking Cohen (1998) and Pfeffer and Sutton (1999) as starting points, the objective of the following sections is to critically discuss the opinions within the existing literature on how to find performance paradoxes, close 'knowing-doing gaps' (term coined by Pfeffer and Sutton 1999), and how to put theoretically formulated strategies into practice.

2.4 Approaching Knowing-Doing Gaps

Several authors (e.g. Gagnon and Michael 2003; Noble and Mokwa 1999; Riel et al. 2009; Semler 1994) have illustrated different approaches to turning knowledge into action and stimulating the 'doing-attitude' of employees. However, before employees can be stimulated to act in a certain way towards

11

strategy implementation, an organisation must first check if its performance suffers from the phenomenon of knowledge being available but not being used to increase performance due to missing implementation (Cohen 1998). Cohen (1998) argues that there is a realistic chance for this phenomenon to appear if four conditions are concurrently present. These conditions are: drifting away from core competencies, using additional resources although the same could be achieved with the existing amount of resources, articulating solutions to a current shortfall by experienced managers, and acting contrary to a course that would improve the performance of an organisation (Cohen 1998). Although the researcher could not find any supportive literature for the first three conditions, the fact that organisations and managers may act contrary to a positive course or their own beliefs is also argued by other authors. While Harvey (1974) cites the inability of managers to come to an agreement responsible for acting contrary to a positive course, Argyris (1982) speaks of a lack of awareness towards what managers think they do and what they are actually doing. A different view, why managers act contrary to their own beliefs is stated by Perrow (1993), who claims that people in general tend to simplify situations and rather long for satisfaction than try to solve a problem as optimal as possible.

Knowing that an organisation possesses all the knowledge necessary to perform better, but is incapable of doing so because it is trapped in the performance paradox (Cohen 1998), opens the floor for several approaches to overcome this hurdle and take action. Cohen (1998) as well as Pfeffer and Sutton (1999) consider it necessary to first of all create an organisational environment in which awareness of the knowing-doing gap is created. However, their approaches to make the management and employees aware of this fact differ. While Cohen (1998) opines that awareness with respect to the above mentioned warning signs needs to be created by conveying urgency, Pfeffer and Sutton (1999) maintain that a shift in the general philosophy of an organisation is necessary to build the framework for an environment which focuses more on action. Instead of scrutinising *how* strategies and techniques are performed, managers shall rather ask themselves *why* they are using them and thereby create a guide to action (Pfeffer and Sutton 1999). Burgelman (1983) and Wooldridge and Floyd (1990) describe this as the need for 'action-managers'. After awareness is created, Cohen (1998) advises to first change all patterns, which are obviously promoting the performance paradox. He speaks of those challenges, which everyone in the organisation knows and are already known for a long time, but which have never been tackled (Cohen 1998). Pfeffer and Sutton (1999) have a different approach to this by discussing a framework for forgiveness within organisations, which is meant to create an environment actively supporting reasoning leaders instead of passive performers. Since many obvious actions are not carried out due to the risk of being punished for a potential failure, this framework should encourage employees to take risks. Additionally, Pfeffer and Sutton (1999) point out that making mistakes is human and wherever actions are carried out there is a chance of failure. Therefore, they call for a forgiving environment, which allows managers to make occasional blunders and likewise stimulates them to act instead of holding their ideas and knowledge back (Pfeffer and Sutton 1999).

Changing the internal environment and framework of an organisation automatically implies that the leaders and managers of this organisation play an essential role in achieving this (House 1971). Nadler and Tushman (1990) maintain that the style of leadership influences the way strategies are implemented. They argue that those leaders and managers, who 'can initiate and implement discontinuous organization change more rapidly

13

and/or prior to the competition have a competitive advantage' (Nadler and Tushman 1990, p.94). However, according to Cohen (1998), many managers play their role poorly and fail in changing the internal environment to the positive or using available opportunities to act because they do not follow their own belief, even if there is minimal risk involved. In order to change this, several authors (e.g. Kotter 2001; Pfeffer and Sutton 1999; Semler 2000) maintain that a proactive approach needs to be followed by the leaders and management. Following this approach would mean that active implementation is perceived as being worth more than having the solution planned on paper and firsthand experience gained by experimenting is worth more than working out theoretical answers (Pfeffer and Sutton 1999). Nadler and Tushman (1990) additionally claim that although a change from a theory driven to a practice driven approach does not necessarily have to be successful, ignoring change and inertia respectively is doomed to failure. Although the opinions of the above mentioned authors differ when it comes to the leadership's tasks, for the purpose of turning knowledge into action, Pfeffer and Sutton (1999, p.104) condense most of the ideas about the right leadership style by stating that 'Leaders create environments, reinforce norms, and help set expectations through what they do, through their actions and not just their words'.

Whereas the above mentioned approaches to turn knowledge into action refer to the implementation of business strategies in general, very little research has been conducted on how performance paradoxes for green strategies can be avoided and knowing-doing gaps for green strategies can be narrowed. Esty and Winston (2009) are the only authors who have thus far conducted research on performance paradoxes and knowing-doing gaps for green strategies. They analysed organisations that have green strategies in place and theoretically formulated but which have not set up a programme of action or an agenda to put these green strategies into practice. Although they acknowledge that every green strategy is unique to a specific business and every organisation will ultimately need a different approach to close the gap between knowing and doing, they suggest a broad agenda which organisations may follow in order to drive environmental thinking into their business operations. They argue that this broad agenda should include short term (0 to 6 months), medium term (6 to 18 months), and long term objectives (18 months and beyond).

The short term objective concentrates on clarifying where the organisation stands regarding its environmental activities, what green strategies need to be implemented, and what and how pilot projects can be launched. In order to achieve this, they maintain that first of all the environmental issues which concern the business need to be analysed by spotting and understanding downside risks and upside opportunities along the value chain. Second, they argue that stakeholders need to be mapped in order to find out what outsiders think of the environmental performance of the organisation. Third, core capabilities need to be assessed and analysis needs to be carried out if the organisation has sufficient and appropriate staff to address its environmental challenges. Apart from these three steps to clarify where the organisation is situated within the environmental realm, Esty and Winston (2009) argue that visible action should follow quickly. They state that organisations should obtain a statement of the chief executive officer (CEO) committing to the environmental values and goals, develop a priority action plan, which addresses the most critical gaps in the organisation's environmental ventures, and execute pilot projects.

While the short term objective concentrates on understanding an organisation's environmental surroundings, the medium term objective focuses on tracking performance and building a culture that facilitates gaining and maintaining an environmental and sustainable competitive advantage. Esty and Winston (2009) state that during this term special attention needs to be paid to five areas. First, the tracking and measurement of all environmental activities should be facilitated and an environmental management system developed which collects information on the performance of suppliers and builds the database for analysing future green strategies. Second, every employee's engagement in and ownership of the organisation's environmental goals should be actively supported by a reflection of the environmental thinking in bonus and performance reviews. Third, communications with critics and advisors from outside the organisation should take place on a regular basis in order to stay updated on environmental developments and avoid environmental myopia. Fourth, internal communication should be encouraged to drive the passion for reaching the environmental goals among staff and create the appropriate morale at the workplace. Fifth, an opportunity should be provided that facilitates meetings between employees from different departments of the organisation to think about the bigger picture and look at drivers, developments, and trends that could recreate entire markets or shift industries.

The long term objective concentrates on embedding environmental activities as a core element into an organisation's corporate strategy. Esty and Winston (2009) argue that three aspects need to be covered in order for this to happen. First, the supply chain needs to be audited in order to indicate potential brand-threatening risks and to understand the own business better. Second, markets need to be re-examined and products refitted by examining whether advantages can be gained from adapting to changing environmental regulations and focussing on new ways to operate more efficiently, improving resource productivity, and reducing cost. Third, stakeholder and partnerships need to be managed to receive a continuous flow of feedback from external sources and enable learning opportunities.

Having discussed how organisations can encourage a more action related behaviour and by reviewing opinions on specific leadership styles supporting a doing attitude, the following section examines what several authors (e.g. Boswell 2006; Caldwell et al. 2004; Gagnon and Michael 2003; Riel et al. 2009) consider as the linchpin of turning knowledge into action. This linchpin is to strategically align those in an organisation with the action-based attitude, which will ultimately be responsible for performing the implementation of a strategy.

2.5 Employee Alignment and Strategy Implementation

All organisations are composed of employees, who are a resource that is valuable, rare, inimitable, and provide an organisation with the basis for sustainable competitive advantage and therefore builds the foundation for every organisation's success (Barney 1991; Colvin and Boswell 2007). Especially when it comes to the successful implementation of organisational strategies, which are vital for an organisation's optimal performance, companies rely on the commitment and capabilities of their employees (Boswell 2006; Noble 1999). However, as several authors have argued (e.g. Argyris 1974; Mintzberg 1978; Nutt 1987) many strategies are not implemented as straightforwardly as planned and fail since they are not accurately understood or immediately accepted by the employees responsible for and affected by the correct implementation (Guth and MacMillan 1986; Mintzberg and Waters 1985). Rapert et al. (2002) maintain that this is due to the fact that in practice, strategies consist of continuously changing and ephemeral decisions which are subject to interpretation and therefore lead to different views of the strategy between

17

executives and functional-level members of the organisation. Skivington and Daft (1991) reinforce this statement by arguing that implementing a strategy demands complex interaction processes between top-level managers and employees. Hence, Rapert et al. (2002) state that the accurate and consistent communication of organisational strategic priorities to functional-level employees is a core competency of the top management.

While the alignment of employees with an organisation's strategy is linked with several difficulties, the existing literature illustrates why organisations should nevertheless strive to achieve the buy-in of their employees and align their staff with their strategic objectives. As an example of the current literature, Gagnon and Michael (2003) point out the increased competitiveness of organisations as the main advantage resulting from strategic employee alignment and argue that the strategic alignment of employees with organisational goals has become a widely adopted technique amongst organisations. Gottschalg and Zollo (2007) go one step further and argue that the alignment between the interests of a collective and an individual generates a sustainable competitive advantage for the organisation. In order to evaluate how organisations can gain this sustainable competitive advantage by aligning their employees with their strategic goals, the following sections will define what aligning employees strategically exactly means and evaluate the key factors and limitations regarding strategic employee alignment.

2.6 Employee Strategic Alignment Defined

Researching the existing literature on the alignment of employees with organisational goals and strategies it can be observed that a large number of authors created and used their own definition for what they understand by employee strategic alignment (Schneider et al. 2003). While Boswell (2006, p.1490) defines the understanding of an organisation's objectives by an employee and how to contribute to these objectives as 'line of sight', Riel et al. (2009, p.1198) define 'on-the-job actions that are aligned with the strategy' as 'strategically aligned behaviour', and Gagnon and Michael (2003, p.25) simply define the understanding, buying-into, and acting upon a certain strategy by employees as 'employee strategic alignment'. Colvin and Boswell (2007) on the other hand split these definitions into two separate ones and define the alignment of an employee's actions with an organisation's strategic goals as 'action alignment' (Colvin and Boswell 2007, p.40) and the alignment of an employee's interests with the strategy of an organisation as 'interest alignment' (Colvin and Boswell 2007, p.44). Following the definition of Gagnon and Michael (2003), regarding the fact that the majority of the currently existing definitions share its tenet and meaning, the understanding and actions of an employee towards an organisation's strategies will in this research project be referred to as 'employee strategic alignment'.

2.7 Reaching Employee Strategic Alignment

The discussion on shaping employee mindsets to support decision-making that are in line with an organisation's objectives has already been led by authors such as Mintzberg (1987) and Weick and Roberts (1993). This discussion was well summarised by Simon (1991, p.32) stating that:

> Doing the job well is not mainly a matter of responding to commands [...]. For the organization to work well, it is not enough for employees to accept commands literally [...]. What is required is that employees take initiative and

19

apply all their skill and knowledge to advance the achievement of the organization's objectives.

While during the late 1980s and early 1990s the discussion was mainly focused on the advantages of employees being aligned with an organisation's strategies, little was discussed and researched about *how* to reach employee strategic alignment. During the late 20th and first decade of the 21st century, several authors (e.g. Boswell 2006; Dell and Kramer 2003; Gagnon and Michael 2003; Noble and Mokwa 1999; Rapert et al. 2002; Riel et al. 2009) devoted their research to the question of *how* organisations can facilitate employees to behave in sync with and contribute to organisational objectives by aligning them with their strategies.

Gagnon and Michael (2003) maintain that before strategic alignment can be achieved, three stages have to be passed. First, the knowledge about the strategy to be implemented needs to be increased, not only around top-level management but also around mid-level management, front-line employees, and everyone else who is involved in the process. They argue that it is of importance that employees do not only know what they are doing but rather understand the overall goal of a strategy. Second, by making the employees understand the strategy and creating interest in its implementation, employees are more likely to act for the purpose of the strategy. Third, by understanding and being interested in the strategy, commitment is created, which is the foundation for strategic alignment (Gagnon and Michael 2003). Noble and Mokwa (1999) also claim that commitment is the cornerstone for a successful implementation. They however argue, in contrast to Gagnon and Michael (2003) that commitment does not only depend on understanding and being interested in the strategy but rather different strategy factors, such as the fit with the organisation's vision, the importance and scope of the strategy, and the support and buy-in by the senior management (Noble and Mokwa 1999). Where most of the authors concur, is the fact that the communication within an organisation, amongst different hierarchical levels, and within hierarchical levels is essential in order to align employees with a strategy and encourage them to take initiative. Boswell (2006) maintains that employees are more likely to contribute to an implementation if they understand their role in an organisation's strategy, which needs to be communicated from the top level of a firm's hierarchy to the bottom. Moreover, Gagnon and Michael (2003) claim that communication is indispensible in order to increase an employee's interest in implementing a strategy. Hambrick and Cannella (1989, p.248) foster this theory by stating that it is 'broad-based selling and communication that must occur to gain support' of all employees involved in a strategy implementation process.

However, employee commitment and alignment is not only created by letting an employee know, what his or her task is with respect to a strategy. Several studies (e.g. Hambrick and Cannella 1989; Noble and Mokwa 1999; Rapert et al. 2002) indicate that there are various kinds of hard and soft factors that have an impact on an employee's degree towards the acceptance of a strategy as well as the degree to which implementation initiatives are taken (Riel et al. 2009). Besser (1995) describes two hard factors which contribute to align employees with an organisation's goals: personal touch money and pay money. He argues that personal touch money, which is given to team leaders in order to organise and support the team's social activities, as well as pay money, in form of performance related bonuses, strengthen the team spirit, promote job security, and give employees a stake in their colleagues' work achievements. 'Combined with equity in benefits and shared feelings of accomplishment, these rewards foster the impression among

21

workers that they will gain if they help the organization succeed' (Besser 1995, p.397). Dell and Kramer (2003) however, state that soft factors are more important than hard factors when it comes to the success of implementation processes. According to Riel et al. (2009), the different soft factors that have an impact on the employee strategic alignment and therefore on the implementation process of a strategy are the employees' perception of motivational efforts, stimulating the development of capabilities, and employee information. They indicate that a positive result with respect to shifting an organisations' knowing into a doing-attitude by aligning employees with its strategy can only be achieved if these factors are utilised jointly, since they build a synergy of stimulation (Riel et al. 2009). Gottschalg and Zollo (2007) concur with this statement by arguing that organisations can facilitate employee strategic alignment through the combined adjustment of the socialisation regime, reward systems, and changes in job design. They indicate that an organisation's strategic goals often result from an 'intense multi-stakeholder dialogue' (Gottschalg and Zollo 2007, p.420) which makes an interest alignment of every involved employee very unlikely. As a consequence, in order to recreate interest alignment, non-aligned employees can be aligned by using a combination of extrinsic (driven by the goal of receiving extrinsic rewards), hedonic (driven by the goal of being engaged in enjoyable, competence enhancing, and self-determined behaviour), and normative (driven by the goal of engaging in behaviour that is compliant with values and norms) motivational practices. As well as Riel et al. (2009) Gottschalg and Zollo (2007) therefore argue that two determinants exist, which have an influence on the motivation of an employee to behave in a certain way. One is the degree to which the behaviour supports the employee to meet their goals and the second determinant is the relevance of each goal to the employee (Gottschalg and Zollo 2007).

Whereas the above mentioned opinions reflect the theory on how employee's mindset can be shaped to support decision-making which is in sync with an organisation's general objectives, Esty and Winston (2009)[1] analysed how employees can be aligned with green strategies in particular. Although the existing literature deals a lot with employee alignment regarding sustainability strategies, Esty and Winston (2009) were found to be the only authors concerning themselves with green strategy alignment in particular. They argue that in order to reach this alignment a certain culture needs to be built which is 'more than just a high-minded mission statement or the words in a CEO's "all-hands" e-mail. It's built day in, day out with a conscious effort and incentives to shape people's behavior' (Esty and Winston 2009, p.207). According to them, organisations which operate under such a green culture use four tools to build it: a vision, reinforced by stretched goals, practices that incorporate green thinking into strategic decision-making, incentives for committing to and engaging in environmental practices, and communications to external and internal audiences.

They state that setting targets that are distinct and concrete, yet far-reaching, allows an organisation to create a vision that facilitates the shaping of employees' mindsets to align them with green strategies. This is because stretching goals illustrates an organisation's long term direction and enables employees in all departments to step up to the challenge. However, operational employees should not be responsible for stretching an organisation's goals since they know more about what actually can be achieved and stretching goals is aimed at going beyond

---

[1] The material in this section draws heavily on the work of Esty and Winston (2009)

what might be realistic at the time the goals are set. Therefore, organisations which want to align their employees with their green strategies should examine what is achievable and then stretch their goals beyond that to evoke creativity, drive innovation, and create an environmental and sustainable competitive advantage.

They further maintain that in addition to stretching the goals, new practices need to be introduced in order to incorporate green thinking in an organisation's decision-making and create a culture that aligns the employees with a firm's green strategies. After analysing companies and their environmental business practices they found that green issues are often hard to quantify which makes straightforward cost benefits analyses complicated. However, they argue that environmental issues play a crucial role in an organisation's decision-making and cost-benefit analyses as payoffs of green initiatives are as real as other business benefits although they might be hard to capture by traditional accounting methods. Therefore, they maintain that the hurdle rate for strategic decision-making needs to be rethought in a way that intangible benefits are not undervalued anymore, giving green projects the opportunity to compete against other projects with hard numbers as benefits in order to create a green culture and align employees with it.

As well as for general employee alignment, incentives also play an important part for committing to and engaging in environmental practices. According to Esty and Winston (2009), successfully operating green organisations drive real employee strategic alignment by developing incentives for environmental success based on specific metrics. They state that 'what gets measured gets managed [and] what people get *paid* for (or promoted for) will get managed even better' (Esty and Winston 2009, p.222). Hence, they maintain that integrating environmental performance into bonuses and compensations will lead to a better employee alignment with green strategies. However, they also claim that if green thinking is already embedded deeply in an organisation's mission, monetary incentives are unnecessary as operating in a non-green way may be interpreted as unacceptable or might lead to jobs being at stake. In addition to the incentives in the form of bonuses and compensations, they further argue that one of the most common methods to align employees with green strategies is to set up award programmes. Since these programmes appeal to an employee's kudos they are known as powerful engagement tools. According to Esty and Winston (2009), employee engagement however needs more than just incentives. Placing environmental ownership on management at operational level and facilitating cross-fertilisation between environmental officials and executives with line responsibilities are further measures to integrate environmental thinking into an organisation's culture and bring employees from different departments on the same level regarding a firm's green strategic decisions.

The fourth tool to create a green culture and align employees strategically with it, is the communication to external and internal audiences. Esty and Winston (2009) maintain that in today's transparent world, spreading the word about green activities and publishing environmental reports gives organisations the opportunity to be seen as responsible corporate citizens and is a powerful tool with which to build trust with all its stakeholders. They state that the content of what is published to the external audience is crucial as it also reflects on the organisation's reputation, which in turn greatly shapes employee identities and influences the internal audience. Surveys show that 92% of all MBA graduates would rather work for a green company and that environmental reporting has an impact on how strong these future employees are aligned with a certain business approach (LaPlante

2004). According to Esty and Winston (2009), honest environmental reporting can signal to all employees what areas they have to focus on, it supports employees in understanding a firm's green perspective, and it builds part of the internal learning process explaining why certain green concepts are seen as a priority and why they are good for the business. As another technique to create a green strategic employee mindset, they illustrate that education and training is an essential part of deeply engaging employees with green strategies. A personal connection to environmental operations can be built by training programmes which focus on topics such as regulatory compliance or efficiency, educate everyone's general knowledge of green business, and train executive officers in seeing the bigger picture of sustainability.

2.8 Limitations to Employee Strategic Alignment

After evaluating the existing literature on employee strategic alignment, it can be observed that researchers primarily devoted themselves to the advantages of an alignment and how to achieve them, while only little is written on the limitations and challenges to employee strategic alignment. However, Colvin and Boswell (2007) point out several downsides and dangers regarding the alignment of employees. They argue that once an organisation has adopted a wrong strategy, aligning employees with this strategy will not have a positive effect on the overall business. Especially, if the alignment of employees with a certain strategy is strong, the danger of Groupthink (Janis 1982) is high which can lead to a loss of employees' ability to identify and recognise the dangers of misdirected strategies. A related drawback of employee strategic alignment may arise if the organisation needs to change or alter its strategy, but due to the strong alignment the ability and willingness of the employees to adapt to the change is diminished, which would result in inflexible staff and failing in altering and changing strategies (Colvin and Boswell 2007). In addition to this, Colvin and Boswell (2007) state that there is a danger of aligning only a part of the employees, which would result in an insider/outsider dynamic, creating an internal chasm between one part of the workforce whose values, actions, and interests are aligned with a strategy and those of the staff whose values, actions, and interests are not aligned with the organisation's strategy. Apart from these drawbacks, there are also costs involved in the strategic alignment of employees. While some costs are direct, for example for personal touch money and pay money, other costs are indirect such as the costs for implementing a less directive supervisory style to change decision-making patterns of employees (Colvin and Boswell 2007).

2.9 Conclusion

In times in which possessing strategic knowledge is not a privilege anymore, mastering the art of implementing strategies rather than formulating them becomes more and more crucial for business success. However, a big gap exists between what organisations know and what they actually do. In order to overcome these performance paradoxes and knowing-doing gaps, several approaches from an organisational and managerial as well as from a green strategic standpoint were discussed. While on an organisational level awareness of the existence of such a gap needs to be created and the organisation's philosophy should be shaped to encourage proactive behaviour, a very big responsibility on a managerial level to create an implementing rather than a knowing work environment lies with the leadership style. If managers and leaders are able to motivate employees, inform them about their role in the strategic process, develop their capabilities, provide a rationale for the strategy, and encourage a climate of open communication, there is a high probability that the overall commitment is higher and strategies are more likely to be implemented than just planned. With respect to green strategies, this action-related attitude can be created by introducing an agenda with short, medium, and long term objectives that identify an organisation's current environmental situation, track environmental performance, and embed green activities into the corporate strategy.

Having defined the role of employee strategic alignment as the linchpin of turning theoretically formulated strategies into action, it can be concluded that organisations are well advised to align their employees with their strategic objectives. By ensuring an uninterrupted communication flow from the top level of an organisation, where the strategic decisions are formulated, to all employees that are affected by or responsible for the implementation of a strategy, the first step is taken to foster shared attitudes, values, and understanding towards the implementation of an organisation's strategy. Especially for aligning employees with green strategies, it is crucial to create an organisational culture in which a green vision is represented by incorporating environmental thinking into strategic decision-making, providing incentives for engaging in green practices, and communicating environmental actions to external and internal audiences. Making effective and well-balanced use of all these factors while keeping in mind that most of them complement each other and in some cases do not work without one another will align employees with the strategic objectives and enable organisations to put theoretically existing strategies into practice.

2.10 Research Questions

Correlating the insights into performance paradoxes, knowing-doing gaps, and employee strategic alignment gained from the existing literature with the background of this research project prompts several research questions. Saunders et al. (2007, p.610) state that a research question is 'One of a number of key questions that the research process will address'. Following this definition and after undertaking Clough and Nutbrown's (2002) Goldilocks test, which analyses if the following research questions are appropriate for investigation at this point in time, by this researcher, and in this setting, the research questions for this research project are as follows:

-   Do knowing-doing gaps and performance paradoxes exist for green strategies?
-   What is the impact of knowing-doing gaps and performance paradoxes on the implementation of green strategies?
-   How can knowing-doing gaps for green strategies be closed and performance paradoxes tackled?
-   To what extent is the outlined existing theory on general strategy implementation applicable to the implementation of green strategies?
-   What role does employee strategic alignment play with regard to the implementation of green strategies compared to general strategies?
-   How can organisations facilitate employee strategic alignment with green strategies?

CHAPTER THREE

RESEARCH METHODOLOGY

3.1 Introduction

Undertaking research is the process of gathering data in order to answer research questions and hence is an instrumental part of reaching the research objective (O'Leary 2005). To reach the objective in a systematic way, this chapter illustrates how the research is carried out and which framework is followed to generate the new knowledge in an effective and scientific manner. This chapter starts by outlining the cornerstone of this framework, the underlying research philosophy. Having laid this foundation for undertaking the primary research, qualitative and quantitative research methodologies are discussed, before a rationale for the chosen methodology is provided and its limitations outlined. To answer the research questions adequately, the research design is determined. This covers issues such as the research strategy, the credibility of research findings, and how the primary data for this project is collected. This chapter closes by outlining the sample under study and illustrating how the primary research data is analysed in order to generate new scientific knowledge in this field of study which provides the basis for the subsequent data analysis chapter.

3.2 Research Philosophy

According to Remenyi et al. (1998), the quality and significance of a research project's outcome mainly depends on the underlying research philosophy. They argue that although several questions such as 'How to research?' and 'What to research?' play a crucial role in answering the research questions, the question 'Why research?' requires special consideration. This is because the answer to this question holds the underlying philosophical perspective for the entire research and builds the foundation for the determination of a suitable research methodology and research design. Burrell and Morgan (1979) state that developing such a philosophical perspective demands making several core assumptions regarding two dimensions: the nature of society and the nature of science. While the sociological dimension requires choosing either a regulatory view or a radical change view, the scientific dimension involves a choice between the two major philosophical approaches to research which are positivism and interpretivism (Burrell and Morgan 1979). Since the development of a society is either seen as arising from the status quo and evolving rationally (regulatory view) or from what can potentially happen in the future due to constant conflict between societal structures (radical change view), the radical change view of society is chosen for this research project (Holden and Lynch 2004). This is because it reflects the diversity and complexity of real world factors that influence the impact of employee strategic alignment on the implementation of green strategies (O'Leary 2005).

As the scientific dimension requires assumptions about the nature of reality, it also determines in which way the research questions are answered and how knowledge is developed (Hudson and Ozanne 1988). In order to select the most appropriate scientific dimension to answer the research questions of this research project, it is essential to consider the differences between the two major philosophical approaches to research: the positivist and interpretivist approach. Several authors (e.g. Holden and Lynch 2004; Hudson and Ozanne 1988; Saunders et al. 2007) maintain that the differences which make these approaches incommensurable lie in their epistemological, ontological, and axiological assumptions. Epistemology is concerned with what constitutes knowledge and what is considered important in a field of study (Saunders et al. 2007). While positivists generate knowledge by using a generalising approach to research and making nomothetic statements, advocates of the interpretivist approach seek to determine reasons, motives, meanings, and other subjective experiences which are context and time-bound (Hudson and Ozanne 1988). Additionally, the view of causality and the research relationship differ amongst these two approaches. While the positivists place a high priority on causal linkages and keep the relationship between the researcher and the subject separated, representatives of the interpretivist approach are of the opinion that the world is too complex to attribute cause and effect. The interpretivists follow a more holistic approach seeing the role of the researcher as being a member of the social reality and therefore view the relationship between the researcher and the subject as interactive (Holden and Lynch 2004).

Besides the epistemological assumptions, the ontological assumptions of the two schools directed towards the nature of reality and the nature of social beings differ. Saunders et al. (2007) argue that positivists assume that one objective reality exists independently of perceptions. Social beings within this reality are mainly characterised as deterministic and reactive. Interpretivists however, deny that only one reality exists and argue that multiple realities exist. They characterise social beings as voluntaristic and proactive, which makes the perception of reality depend on how it is perceived mentally and subjectively (Hudson and Ozanne 1988). The third major aspect which differentiates the positivist from the interpretivist approach is their underlying goal or axiology. While the goal of the positivists is to generalise findings and establish universal applicable laws in order to make future predictions, the goal of the interpretivist approach is to understand the behaviour of the research subject and to 'see the world from an insider's perspective' (Hudson and Ozanne 1988, p.511).

Despite the fact that the nature of philosophy and its influence on the way knowledge is generated is a major philosophical dispute, and hence no single view on these different philosophies is seen as unequivocally correct, a certain philosophical position needs to be chosen to reflect the research objective (Holden and Lynch 2004; Hughes and Sharrock 1997). Selecting a certain research philosophy is central to the question 'How to research?' as well as to the question 'What to research?' since it is a crucial parameter to answering the question 'Why research?'. Therefore, this research project chooses its underlying research philosophy based on the research objective as well as the research questions (Holden and Lynch 2004). As the research questions of this project aim at understanding the behaviour of employees towards a company's alignment with green strategies rather than generating universally applicable laws, an interpretivist approach is chosen. Further aspects which speak in favour of an interpretivist approach are the time-bound as well as context-dependent knowledge generation, and the willingness to determine reasons, motives, meanings, and other subjective experiences in order to understand why and how knowing-doing gaps with respect to green strategies exist and how they can be closed (Hudson and Ozanne 1988).

Due to the fact that the topic under research is highly complex and of a multi-faceted nature, the interpretivist philosophic view with its more holistic approach suits the research objective more. This is because the relationship between the subject under study and the researcher is seen as interactive rather than separated (Holden and Lynch 2004). The fact that social beings are characterised as voluntaristic and proactive under the interpretivist approach, rather than deterministic and reactive, qualifies the interpretivist philosophy for the purpose of this research project. The existing literature on this topic mainly views it from this perspective as well (e.g. Besser 1995; Esty and Winston 2009; Gagnon and Michael 2003; Hambrick and Cannella 1989).

3.3 Qualitative Versus Quantitative Research Methodology

Having answered the question 'Why research?' by determining a suitable philosophy for this research project, subsequently an adequate research methodology needs to be determined in order to answer the question about 'How to research?'. Generally, the literature distinguishes between two different major research methodologies: the qualitative and quantitative research methodology (Denzin and Lincoln 2000; Malhotra and Birks 1999; Silverman 1998). The perception of which of these primary data collection methods provides the most accurate understanding of the research topic, determines whether a qualitative or quantitative methodology is used (Malhotra and Birks 1999). Although both methodologies are established and qualified to generate primary data, they are rooted in fundamentally different basic assumptions which is why it is important to the research to be aware of these differences and to decide to follow either the qualitative or the quantitative methodology (Malhotra and Birks 1999). 'Qualitative researchers stress the socially constructed nature of reality, the intimate relationship between the researcher and what is studied, and the situational constraints that shape inquiry' (Denzin and Lincoln 1994, p.4), which emphasises the value-laden nature of inquiry and seeks to answer questions regarding social experiences. In contrast, quantitative researchers 'emphasize the measurement and analysis of causal relationships between variables, not processes [...] within a value-free framework' (Denzin and Lincoln 1994, p.4). Becker (1993) further maintains that qualitative research differs from quantitative research in five ways: use of positivism, acceptance of postmodern sensibilities, capturing the individual's point of view, examining the constraints of everyday life, and securing rich descriptions.

According to Malhotra (2004), these differences result in different objectives and outcomes of research. He states that the goal of qualitative research is to gain an understanding of the underlying motivations and its outcome is to develop initial understanding. The objective of the quantitative approach however, is to quantify the data and generalise the outcomes from the sample to the rest of the population to recommend a final course of action (Malhotra 2004). Furthermore, Malhotra argues that the sample in qualitative research is a small number of unrepresentative cases whereas a large number of representative cases serves the quantitative methodology as a sample. Regarding the data, he argues that qualitative researchers collect data in an unstructured way and analyse it non-statistically, while quantitative researchers follow a structured data collection process and analyse the data statistically (Malhotra 2004). These fundamental differences lead to an ongoing discussion between proponents of the two methodologies. While quantitative researchers dismiss qualitative studies, arguing that their findings are not valid because they are based on one single case only, qualitative researchers reject statistical and other quantitative methods because these techniques are not sensitive enough to capture feelings, motives, attitudes, and behaviour of people (Malhotra and Birks 1999). For the purpose of this research project the qualitative methodology is applied, because it has been used for similar research projects to investigate the behaviour and impact of employees towards strategic alignment and green strategies (e.g. Argyris 1982; Cohen 1998; Esty and Winston 2009; Hambrick and Cannella 1989; Mintzberg 1978; Pfeffer and Sutton 1999).

3.4 Rationale for Qualitative Research Methodology

The qualitative research methodology is used for the purpose of this research project for several reasons. Firstly, qualitative research is seen as an unstructured and primarily exploratory approach, which is based on small samples and intends to provide insight and understanding (Malhotra and Birks 1999). This makes qualitative research an appropriate methodology for the overarching interpretivist philosophy as it is often directly associated with its subjective and holistic approach (Silverman 1998). In addition, Silverman (1998) states that the interpretivist philosophy is often applied within the context of work routines, which is of special interest for this research project regarding green work routines and which requires a qualitative research methodology as it uses interviews to understand the underlying phenomena.

Despite the fact that the qualitative methodology suits the chosen research philosophy, there are several other reasons that justify the choice of qualitative over quantitative research for this project. Malhotra and Birks (1999) maintain that qualitative research is used if the research information is sensitive, if subconscious feelings are involved, if complex phenomena are investigated, and if the research is aimed at creating a holistic dimension. They state that interviewees might be unwilling to provide right or honest answers to specific questions that have a negative impact on their ego or status or invade their privacy. Especially when interview questions relate to corporate performance and plans, which includes employee strategic alignment and strategy implementation, qualitative techniques and interviews are powerful tools to create trust and allow the researcher to get close to the interviewees in order to access sensitive data (Malhotra and Birks 1999). As subconscious feelings, values, and emotions play a vital role when analysing the truth behind knowing-doing gaps and performance paradoxes, researchers need to approach these with the help of qualitative measures. Malhotra and Birks (1999) point out that interviewees are often unable to answer correctly to questions that tap their subconscious, because their feelings, values, and emotions are disguised by rationalism or other defence mechanisms, which can only be overcome by using qualitative research.

Furthermore, the use of qualitative research is justified by the fact that this research project investigates a complex phenomenon, involving multiple social and economic factors, which may be difficult to capture with structured questions and hence require a qualitative approach (Malhotra and Birks 1999). Malhotra and Birks (1999, p.135) additionally argue that in order to gain a holistic outlook that provides a complete and comprehensive picture of the impact of employee alignment on the implementation of green strategies, qualitative interviewing allows the researcher to build up 'an understanding of the interrelationship of the context'. This allows the researcher to cover the interconnectedness of several components of the phenomenon within this research project. Halfpenny (1979) emphasises the rationale stated by Malhotra and Birks (1999) by maintaining that the features of qualitative research are flexibility, speculation, subjectivity, and the softness of the topic under study. The very nature of the qualitative interview technique allows the researcher to cover these features and provide the most accurate understanding of the research topic.

In addition to the outlined rationale for using a qualitative approach for this research project, Denzin and Lincoln (2000) provide another argument why a qualitative methodology is more appropriate than a quantitative one. They state that a quantitative methodology stresses the analysis and measurement of causal relationships between variables rather than processes and advocates of this methodology claim to work within a value-free framework. Qualitative researchers however, emphasise the socially constructed nature of reality within their methodology which is accompanied by a value-laden nature of inquiry. Moreover, the word *qualitative* implies an emphasis on the qualities of entities and on processes and meaning that are not examined or measured (if measured at all) in terms of quantity, amount, intensity, or frequency' and that the qualitative researcher 'seek answers to questions that stress *how* social experiences is created and given meaning' (Denzin and Lincoln 2000, p.8). As the research project seeks to understand the various ways in which the strategic alignment of social beings is connected to the successful implementation of green strategies and the existence of knowing-doing gaps rather than explain causal relationships, a qualitative methodology is more applicable. Although proponents of the quantitative methodology argue that qualitative research is biased, relies on empathetic identification, and does not guarantee understanding, qualitative research 'involves an interpretive, naturalistic approach to the world [and studies] things in their natural settings, attempting to make sense of, or to interpret, phenomena in terms of the meanings people bring to them' (Denzin and Lincoln 2000, p.3). Therefore, this methodology is more appropriate for the purpose of this research project than the quantitative methodology.

3.5 Limitations to Qualitative Research

Despite the fact that qualitative research suits the research project better than quantitative research, there are some limitations to this research methodology which need to be considered. According to Denzin and Lincoln (2000), the findings resulting from qualitative research cannot be extended to wider populations with the same degree of certainty as can the findings of quantitative research. This is due to the fact that qualitative findings are not tested to discover whether they are statistically significant or due to chance (Denzin and Lincoln 2000). In addition to that, Silverman (1998) argues that the qualitative methodology aims at understanding the perception of the stakeholders, in this case the interviewees, which makes the research process subjective. Therefore, the analysis and findings of a qualitative research project depend heavily on the skills of the researcher, interviewing the respondents and analysing the gathered data (Silverman 1998). Additionally, the quality of the findings differs if the researcher is biased and if the researcher influences the respondents' quality and quantity of information in any way (Mason 2002).

3.6 Research Design

Knowing the applied research philosophy and methodology, the research design builds the framework for conducting the research project and determines the details of the procedures necessary for gathering the information (Malhotra and Birks 1999). One part of building this framework is specifying a suitable research approach. Generally, two research approaches are distinguished: deduction and induction. The deductive approach is mainly characterised by first developing a theory and then testing the hypothesis. During the inductive approach the data is first collected before a theory is developed based on the data analysis (Saunders et al. 2007). The deductive approach generally follows a more positivistic philosophy by putting more emphasis on scientific principles, explaining causal relationships, and collecting quantitative data. As the inductive approach stresses the close understanding of the research context and meanings humans attach to events, as well as the collection of qualitative data, the inductive approach suits the underlying research questions, research philosophy, and research methodology of this project better than the deductive approach and is therefore used (Saunders et al. 2007).

In addition to the research approach, the purpose of the research is an essential part of the research design. According to Saunders et al. (2007), the purpose of research and thereby the answers to the research questions can either be exploratory, descriptive, or explanatory. Since the research project aims at gaining new insights with respect to employee alignment and green strategies as well as finding out how the implementation of green strategies is affected by the knowing-doing gap, the purpose of this project is exploratory rather than descriptive or explanatory (Robson 2002).

3.6.1 Research Strategy

Beyond the research approach and purpose, Saunders et al. (2007) state that collecting primary data requires a certain research strategy. They maintain that researchers may chose between using experiments, surveys, case studies, action research, ethnography, and archival research as suitable research strategies. Since ethnography is rooted in the inductive approach and its 'purpose is to describe and explain the social world [as well as] to gain insights about a particular context and better understand and interpret it from the perspective(s) of those involved' (Saunders et al. 2007, p.142) it suits the purpose of the research project. Although the ethnographic research strategy originally involved observations, today it encompasses a much broader spectrum, allowing the researcher to work with this strategy without making observations at first hand but using in-depth interviews instead (Malhotra and Birks 1999).

3.6.2 Time Horizon and Credibility of Research Findings

Another important issue with respect to planning this research project and the corresponding research design is the question about the time horizon. According to Saunders et al. (2007), the time horizon can either be cross-sectional or longitudinal. They argue that cross-sectional projects study a specific phenomenon at a particular point in time, whereas longitudinal projects observe events or employees over a longer time period. As one of the goals of the cross-sectional perspective is to explain and elucidate the occurrence of phenomena and paradoxes, it is the selected perspective for this project. Taking this perspective facilitates the understanding of performance paradoxes, know-doing gaps, and the role of employees within this context for a certain point in time whereas the time constraint of this research project precludes a longitudinal perspective (Creswell 1994).

The credibility of research findings is another crucial aspect for every research project. In order to ensure that the outcomes and conclusions stand up to scrutiny and to decrease the chance of providing wrong answers to the research questions, special attention needs to be paid to the reliability and validity of a project (Raimond 1993). As qualitative analysis is especially prone to unreliability due to participant errors and bias as well as observer errors and bias, the following three overarching questions have to be kept in mind during the data collection and analysis of this research project (Robson 2002). Asking 'Will the measures yield the same results on other occasions?', 'Will similar observations be reached by other observers?', and 'Is there transparency in how sense was made from the raw data?' during the data collection and analysis facilitates the provision of consistent research findings and the reduction of wrong answers (Easterby-Smith et al. 2002, p.53). Validity throughout the project means that observations, identifications, and measurements which are made during the research process are what the research project says they are. This is achieved by creating transparency of the research techniques and analysis tools used (Mason 2002).

3.6.3 Qualitative Interviews

The collection of the primary data for this research project is achieved by conducting qualitative interviews. Qualitative interviews are a purposeful discussion between two or more people and are one of the most powerful ways to understand the impact of employees on strategy implementation (Denzin and Lincoln 2000; Kahn and Cannell 1957). As trust needs to be created for this research project in order to request sensitive or confidential information, undertaking qualitative interviews is seen as the most appropriate data collection technique (Saunders et al. 2007). The existing literature distinguishes between three different qualitative interview techniques: structured interviews, semi-structured interviews, and unstructured interviews (Denzin and Lincoln 2000; Malhotra and Birks 1999; Mason 2002; Saunders et al. 2007). Structured interviews are characterised by using a set of standardised questions, which limits the social interaction between the interviewee and the interviewer (Saunders et al. 2007). Semi-structured interviews on the other hand are non-standardised and follow a set of themes and questions to be covered, which may vary from interview to interview to explore topics in further detail (Denzin and Lincoln 2000). Unstructured or in-depth interviews, sometimes also referred to as open-ended ethnographic interviews, are informal and non-standardised. They are used to explore a specific topic in-depth, whereby the interviewer is given the freedom to talk about the topic under study in a non-directive manner (Saunders et al. 2007). As in-depth interviews are used in exploratory research projects to understand complex behaviour of employees and they may uncover underlying motivations, beliefs, and attitudes towards the implementation of green strategies, four one-hour in-depth interviews are conducted in order to collect the primary data for the subsequent analysis (Denzin and Lincoln 2000; Saunders et al. 2007).

Despite the above mentioned rationale for conducting in-depth interviews there are several advantages and challenges regarding this interview technique which need to be considered during the research process. Malhotra and Birks (1999) maintain that in-depth interviews have four major advantages. They state that first of all, in-depth interviews are more likely to uncover greater depth of insights than focus groups due to the interviewer's ability to concentrate on the individual interviewee. Secondly, responses can be directly attributed to the respondent. Third, free exchange of information is possible due to the absence of social pressure to conform to group responses, which allows gathering sensitive data. Fourth, in-depth interviews are easier to arrange than other methods such as focus groups. However, Malhotra and Birks (1999) also point out several challenges regarding in-depth interviews. They argue that the obtained data is difficult to interpret and analyse and that the length of in-depth interviews is often limited by cost factors and the available time of the interviewee.

As in-depth interviews are generally more unstructured than straightforward questionnaires, they are also more complex and harder to plan and conduct (Mason 2002). In order to generate relevant data from the in-depth interviews, the interviewer therefore has to act quickly, coherently, and effectively upon the situations evolving during the interview in a way that is consistent with the research questions (Mason 2002). Hence, Mason's (2002) seven step approach is followed to plan and conduct the interviews. This approach 'orchestrate[s] an interaction which moves easily and painlessly between topics and questions [and assesses on the spot] the relevance of each part of the interaction' to the research questions by considering the scope and sequence as well as substance and style of the interview questions (Mason 2002, p.73). Furthermore, the interviews are planned and conducted by relating to the interviewees' circumstances and experiences, using an appropriate language and style (Saunders et al. 2007). Another focus is directed towards asking open, probing, and unbiased questions in a neutral tone and ensuring an accurate active listening (Saunders et al. 2007). To avoid bias and facilitate later queries with respect to responses and direct quotes of the respondents, a Dictaphone is used as the method of recording the interviews, with the permission being asked from interviewees prior to the interview. The advantages of this recording method are, amongst others, that the interviewer can concentrate more on the questioning and listening and that an accurate and unbiased record of information is provided, which allows direct quotes to be used (Saunders et al. 2007). Typical disadvantages of tape recording the interviews are that it may adversely affect the interaction between interviewer and respondents, it may reduce the interviews' reliability due to inhibition of responses, and technical problems may occur (Saunders et al. 2007).

3.7 Sampling

After designing the research, an appropriate sample for the investigation needs be determined. According to Mason (2002), sampling is the principle and procedure to identify, choose, and gain access to relevant data sources from which data will be generated using the prior determined methodology. The purpose of the sample is therefore to provide access to data that allows the development of an empirically and theoretically grounded argument about the role of employee strategic alignment in the implementation of green strategies (Mason 2002). As the sample must relate meaningfully to the universe of this project, the sample must be information rich (Patton 1990). To achieve this richness and to make the sample representative, the interview partners have to have knowledge and experience in the area under study, the ability to reflect, the time to be interviewed, the willingness to participate, and they need to be articulate (Morse 1986, 1991). Mason (2002) illustrates three sampling strategies to identify the right interview partners and to develop the above mentioned theoretically and empirically grounded argument. Depending on the research objective and the underlying research questions one can choose between a representational, evocative, or strategic sampling strategy (Mason 2002). Whereas representational sampling is a strategy used to represent a wider population or universe, evocative sampling seeks to provide an example of how it could represent a wider population without claiming how well it represents that universe. For this research project, the strategic sampling strategy is chosen as one of its underlying strategies is theoretical sampling, which interpretivists use to explain certain phenomena such as knowing-doing gaps and performance paradoxes (Malhotra and Birks 1999). The theoretical sampling further encapsulates a relevant range in relation to the wider universe and is used for constructing a sample that is theoretically and empirically meaningful to develop theories and arguments with respect to the topic of this research project (Glaser and Strauss 1967). Using this method and considering the underlying ontological perspective of this project, people and their experiences, feelings, behaviours, and practices constitute the research sample (Denzin and Lincoln 2000). Due to the time limitations of this project, four people are interviewed. As the key issue of qualitative sampling is how to focus strategically and meaningfully, it is more important that these four interviewees provide access to enough data and with the right focus than providing a representation of the entire universe. Considering the interpretive logic, which evaluates and questions different ways of classifying people regarding the topic under study, one front-line employee, two middle managers, and one executive director from one of the world's largest electricity company are interviewed in-depth. Choosing these employees allows the evaluation of different hierarchical levels from several perspectives to cover the comprehensiveness of the research objective and to answer the underlying research questions. Gathering information on the opinions, experiences, practices, and behaviours of these employees additionally contributes to increasing the analytical validity and authenticity as it ensures the analysis of the research objective from different angles. Thereby, the sample enables the researcher to analyse the bigger picture as well as assess a detailed picture from different hierarchical levels (Mason 2002).

3.8 Analysis of the Research

To ensure that the collected data from the sample is useful, it needs to be analysed and its meaning understood (Saunders et al. 2007). Therefore, an analysis of the data needs to be performed that provides a persuasive argument or explanation on the basis of the qualitative data (Mason 2002). Generally, four categories of qualitative data analysis strategies are distinguished: understanding the characteristics of language, discovering regularities, comprehending the meaning of text or action, and reflection (Tesch 1990). Whereas the first two categories represent deductive and highly structured approaches that follow a set of predetermined procedures, the last two categories represent inductive approaches (Saunders et al. 2007). This

47

research project follows the grounded theory, which is an inductively-based analytical procedure, as it seeks to build up a theory that is adequately grounded in the collected data by using an inductive approach (Strauss and Corbin 1998). Using the grounded theory combines the strengths of Tesch's (1990) two inductive strategies of comprehending the meaning of text or action and reflection allowing the comprehension and management of the collected data. Furthermore, it facilitates the transformation of the collected data by integrating related data from different transcripts, indentifying key themes and patterns, developing theories, and drawing and verifying conclusions (Dey 1993; Miles and Huberman 1994). To achieve this and to analyse the researched data systematically and accurately, the data is first categorised. Afterwards the data is unitised (open coding) and relationships are recognised (axial coding). Then theories are developed and tested (selective coding) in order to reach conclusions (Saunders et al. 2007; Strauss and Corbin 1998). While the categorisation provides an analytical framework to pursue the analysis, unitising the data attaches relevant units of data to the appropriate categories (Saunders et al. 2007). Recognising relationships between these units facilitates finding key themes and patterns or relationships within the data which allows developing and testing hypotheses (Dey 1993; Miles and Huberman 1994; Silverman 1993). Additionally, the grounded theory uses the concept of theoretical sampling. Using this concept, 'sampling is purposive [and] critical cases are chosen to further the development of concepts and categories being used, so as to aid the process of developing an emerging theory that will be thoroughly grounded in that data' (Saunders et al. 2007, p.499). As this concept continues until new data is revealed that is relevant to the topic under study, which is also known as theoretical saturation, and hence suits the chosen research methodology, it is applied for this research project (Strauss and Corbin 1998).

3.9 Conclusion

To reach the research objective and to answer the research questions in a systematic and scientific way, this chapter introduced a research framework that aligns the underlying research instruments and viewpoints with the topic under study and thereby facilitates a suitable method of primary data collection. Derived from the topic under study, an interpretivist approach is adopted as a research philosophy which, in combination with the characteristics of the research objective, leads to the use of a qualitative methodology. Under this methodology, a research design was created that follows an inductive approach with an exploratory focus and makes use of in-depth interviews to collect the primary data. To ensure that the collected data comes from a relevant source, the sample consists of four employees who represent different hierarchical levels of the organisation. With this sample providing access to data that allows the development of an empirically and theoretically grounded argument about the role of employee strategic alignment in the implementation of green strategies, this chapter provides the theoretical framework for the following analysis of the data.

CHAPTER FOUR

FINDINGS AND ANALYSIS

4.1 Introduction

The following sections outline the research findings and analysis based on four in-depth interviews and the aforementioned research methodology. The interviews were conducted in the electricity company's headquarters and lasted an average duration of one hour during which insights into green strategy implementation and employee strategic alignment were gained. The generated data is divided into three main categories, which are further split into several sub-categories. The three main categories are: Implementation of Green Strategies, Employee Strategic Alignment, and Reaching Employee Strategic Alignment. Although some categories and sub-categories are closely interlinked and cannot be considered as stand-alone categories or sub-categories, this categorisation is chosen in order to enable a systematic approach to analyse the data, compare it to the literature, and answer the corresponding research questions.

4.2 Electricity Company and Interviewee Backgrounds

The electricity company under study was founded in the early 19th century as a statutory corporation. From then on, it evolved into a leading electricity company in its country, which is engaged in electricity generation, distribution, and supply. 95% of it is owned by the Government, while the remaining shares are held by an employee share option trust (Datamonitor 2009). Operating mainly in its own country the organisation has several divisions that operate independently in the electricity market. In total the electricity company employs approximately 8,000 people.

As this electricity company has a long history in developing and implementing green and sustainable business strategies, it meets the criteria to be suitable to this research project and to provide the source for primary data in order to answer the research questions. The experience of the employees with green strategies, having undergone a shift from an organisation without a green focus to an organisation that is committed to leadership in carbon management and energy efficiency, make this electricity company an appropriate organisation to conduct the in-depth interviews with for this research project. To benefit from this experience and to provide a holistic view on the interaction between different hierarchical levels, one front-line employee, two middle managers, and one executive director are interviewed. Their job descriptions and responsibilities are as follows:

Interviewee 1 is an engineer and represents the hierarchical level of front-line employees. His responsibilities are, amongst others, the implementation of green strategies in for the power stations. Interviewee 2 is a manager for sustainability projects, who reports to the executive director of sustainability and together with Interviewee 3 represents the hierarchical level of middle managers. His job is to develop and run a change programmes in order to embed awareness of sustainability within the culture of the organisation. Interviewee 3 is a health and environment manager. He works on green strategies as well as environment related projects and reports to the executive director for sustainability. Interviewee 4 is the executive director for sustainability. He is one of six directors that report to the chief executive and represents the hierarchical level of executive directors.

4.3 Research Findings

In order to answer the research questions the interviewees were asked questions about the implementation of green strategies, employee strategic alignment, and reaching employee strategic alignment within their company and area of work. The findings resulting from the interviews regarding these main categories and their sub-categories are as follows:

4.3.1 Implementation of Green Strategies – Differences between Green and General Strategies

In order to determine the impact of employee strategic alignment on the implementation of green strategies to develop explanatory theory for closing knowing-doing gaps, it is essential to firstly evaluate the differences between the implementation of green and general strategies. Independently of their hierarchical level, all interviewees state that there are no differences between the implementation of a green and a general strategy regarding the use of a fixed approach or framework. Interviewee 2 states that '[the implementation of a green strategy] depends on the time schedule, the strategic elements, the input of reviewers' and does not explicitly make a difference between approaches that are applied for green or general strategies. Interviewee 4 concurs with this statement by answering the question if the organisation utilises distinct approaches for green strategies with a simple 'No. No'.

The interviewees state that green strategies are often approached in the same way as general strategies. Interviewee 4 outlines that 'you look at your strategies and you adapt to what your environment is now telling you' referring to their new strategic framework, which was launched in 2008 and has an environmental focus. The approach of adapting to the evolving environmental circumstances of the company which is used for general as well as green strategies is also addressed by Interviewee 2. He says 'we don't expect it to be there forever [... it is] a process of confrontation and iteration', referring to one of their green strategies that they adapt to the current circumstances on a yearly basis. As their strategic planning has become more complex due to the focus on a green strategy and achieving compliance with upcoming legislations, Interviewee 3 states that they 'are moving back towards strategic planning' after having abolished it 'but that may all change again in a short while'.

Although none of the interviewees explicitly differentiates between approaches or frameworks for the implementation of green and general strategies, they show a considerable difference regarding the purpose of the implementation. Interviewee 2 summarises the statements of all interviewees by saying that:

> A key differentiator is that you start looking at not just the financial bottom line. You are looking at other indicators. So you are saying: the company's aim now is not just to make profit, but the company's aim is to do so in an environmental way and we are now concerned, not just with the products of the company, but we are concerned with the wider environmental impact of everything that we do and the organisations we interact with, the products we buy etc. So that has become a different focus. [...] It places the company more clearly in its environment. I suppose it makes the company think about social responsibility. [...] You could say that the company strategy is a green strategy. And there is no other strategy in this company. It is overarching. There is an overarching vision for the company saying that our organisation will be commercially successful and a leading electrical utility with sustainability embedded in the culture of the

company. So that guides all the strategy of the company. You start from that statement.

Hence, in the case of this electricity company, following a green strategy can only be successful if it overarches all other strategies and at the same time is deeply embedded within the mindsets of the employees. This allows the green strategy to become a universal basis for everything that is accomplished within the organisation and puts it in a more holistic setting.

Beyond that, following a green strategy is indicative for the future of the organisation as the announcement and communication of it provides a clearer message and direction for the employees. Interviewee 4 outlines this by stating that:

> I'd say that the very announcement of the new green strategy was very well received in the company. It was clear, it was simple and clear. It wasn't complex [...] – people loved it. You have all the growth strategies and profit and ... you know ... competition and all ... but this is kind of more compelling, this is more visionary. [...] It is a compelling story. It is a liked story. It is liked by our people and it is liked externally. It is a good story. We are in a much better place than we were two years ago, because we've got this higher level goal kind of thing.

For some employees, implementing green strategies instead of general strategies even opens new incentives for following this strategy. Interviewee 1 argues that 'even if I would have no interest in sustainability, I would be starting to get into it, because from a career point of view [...] it certainly adds something to your skill set [...] and it can significantly enhance careers'.

The fact that the electricity company's compelling green strategy is overarching, as well as their endeavour to embed it deeply into everyone's day-to-day operations, allows for another difference between green and general strategies. While general strategies are

55

normally communicated top-down, Interviewee 1 states that front-line employees are more involved in green strategies and make bottom-up strategies possible. Answering the question about how green strategies are introduced to him he says:

> I suppose an example would be the electric vehicle. That was a strategy started from the CEO and we are now buying electric cars in our stations. But it came also back from the bottom of the stations saying: 'We want more electric cars' and things like that. So it was coming from both directions, but starting from the top.

Having these insights into similarities and differences between green and general strategies and being aware of the possibility of bottom-up strategies, the findings on the existence of knowing-doing gaps and performance paradoxes with respect to green strategies are presented below.

4.3.2 Implementation of Green Strategies – Knowing-Doing Gaps and Performance Paradoxes

When asked if knowing-doing gaps or performance paradoxes exist with respect to their green strategies, interviewees from all hierarchical levels seem to agree that those phenomena are present, irrespectively of the type of strategy. Interviewee 4 states that 'the implementation of a strategy is never clean [...] it's just the way it is. So you might, as a result from that, have to adjust your target in some area and create a different target in a different place, maybe more stretching a target'. Interviewee 1 concurs by saying that 'People know how to do things the old way. They don't want to surrender that control and they are threatened, maybe, by new things coming in' and refers to the launch of a new green strategy.

Discussing the existence of knowing-doing gaps and performance paradoxes the front-line employee and the executive director both highlight that these phenomena mainly appear within the middle management of the company. The executive director outlines that front-line employees and directors might be more concerned about the implementation of green strategies and reports:

> We've almost bypassed the management. Just kind of unusual in a way. So the management then has its targets from their bosses, from the top. And the targets are about profits and delivering numbers [...]. So our challenge now: we have a change programme in place about mobilising the minds and hearts of the managers and embedding the sustainability targets in their targets but also in their hearts so that they line up with what's going on on the ground.

Regarding initiatives to close knowing-doing gaps and reduce performance paradoxes, Interviewee 2 argues that 'You find that with a green strategy you get a percentage of people who are highly motivated because they believe it. They identify with it [but] it would be wrong to assume that the majority of people are motivated in the same way'. This illustrates the potential for narrowing knowing-doing gaps and reducing the chance of performance paradoxes as more employees are generally highly motivated when working on a green strategy. Interviewee 2 identifies this as a critical success factor and says:

> And in fact this gap gives you the task, doesn't it? You have to recognise that in order to make things happen, you got to have targets, you got to review those targets, you got to keep at it, you got to assume that there will be an initial wave of enthusiasm, and you got to assume that's going to die back and people reverse and you have to put additional work in, you are going to do a new thing.

He further compares this phenomenon to a spinning top, adding:

It is like spinning a top and it will spin. You say: 'That's great. That is a proper spinning' but it will slow down. So you have to give it the next impetus. So that's the thing: people will always reverse to their habitual ways. The idea in the culture change is to make the sustainable way their habitual way.

Incorporating this thought, Interviewee 3 summarises the findings on the existence and occurrence of knowing-doing gaps and performance paradoxes by saying that it is 'depending on the type of company, the type of management within the company, the way management is aligned behind a particular strategy, [and] leadership direction'. He further maintains that in order to prevent these phenomena from happening 'You need always to ensure that the employees are aligned with the overall strategy and that is why we did this culture change in terms of engaging people into things'. Having determined that employee strategic alignment plays a significant role in narrowing knowing-doing gaps and reducing performance paradoxes leads to the findings on employee strategic alignment.

4.3.3 Employee Strategic Alignment – Its Role in Green Strategy Implementation

According to the interviewees, employee strategic alignment plays a significant role with regard to the implementation of green strategies. The importance of achieving employee strategic alignment is well known throughout all hierarchical levels as well as the need to communicate green strategies and their goals in order to obtain employee buy-in for a successful implementation. The executive director outlines that his company tries to 'infiltrate the decision-making processes and to inject the sustainability dimension to every decision that we make'. One example which illustrates the meaning of employee strategic alignment for the electricity company is the transfer of responsibility and the involvement of employees within decision-making processes. The front-line employee states that 'there is one sustainability champion in every station, who is responsible for the sustainability improvement plan'. Furthermore, Interviewee 2 comments on the importance of the alignment and adds that employees are asked during internal surveys if the goals of their green strategies are realistic. The results of these surveys are directly reported to the executive director team and have an impact on strategic targets for the upcoming years.

The effort that is made to strategically align employees within the company is also manifested in the statement of one of the middle managers and the front-line employee that they and more and more of their colleagues are aligned. According to Interviewees 1 and 2, this is due to the numerous communication initiatives such as the internal newsletter, internal e-zines, internal surveys, and internal competition with respect to reaching green targets. However, the role of employee strategic alignment is not only important for the implementation of green strategies. The successful implementation is also of importance for the employee strategic alignment. Interviewee 4 states that implementing green strategies 'fulfils a higher need in people to be part of something that is more noble' which illustrates synergy effects between employee strategic alignment and the implementation of green strategies.

Although the interviews revealed the important role of employee strategic alignment in green strategy implementation, the extent to which all employees might be able to be aligned is debatable. Interviewee 1 states that 'I think it comes down to personality types. Some people aren't really interested in strategy or anything like that, but can still be very good at what they do. Other people are very strategic and have to know all the details'. Interviewee 2 points out that he 'would expect that people at a lower level wouldn't have the same level of understanding and wouldn't need to have the same level of understanding and the detail [...], but all they need to do is to understand what it means to them and their line of business'.

4.3.4 Employee Strategic Alignment – The Differences between Green and General Strategies

One of the main differences that distinguishes employee strategic alignment with green strategies from an alignment with general strategies, is the willingness among the employees to be aligned with a green strategy. Interviewee 2 summarises the statements of the interviewees by saying that:

> When we did the staff survey, we found that 25% of the people would put themselves in the process of being interested [...] it gave you a very big base to start with. [...] So it is great to have that level of enthusiasm. Now, with another strategy, you wouldn't have that. So that is where a green strategy implementation is different [...], because you've that group of people with personal commitment.

All four interviewees state that they are personally more committed to a green strategy and think that their colleagues are as well. Particularly among front-line employees, the enthusiasm about and engagement in green strategies is remarkably high compared to general strategies. Interviewee 2 states that his company launched an award scheme competition with an environmental focus and received 200 entries while only 30-40 were expected.

However, Interviewee 1 argues that 'if you introduce something new like sustainability, people don't really know anything about it. There is resistance. There is cynicism'. He points out that it is very likely that there will be employees who are reluctant to change and that people in general like to take a contrarian view on new strategies. Although it is unlikely that every single employee will be aligned with a green strategy, employees' alignment with a green strategy compared to the alignment to a general strategy has several advantages. According to all four interviewees, the strategic alignment with the new green strategy leads to increased enthusiasm, pride, and happiness among themselves and their colleagues. Furthermore, a boost in morale was identified by Interviewee 3 once the green strategy was launched and employees are identifying themselves more with the values that a green strategy represents, which leads to personal fulfilment. Interviewee 2 states that in addition to this, 'it is easier in general to motivate people if they believe that what they are doing is right and is of value to themselves, the community, the families'. Therefore, and because of the remarkable enthusiasm and engagement from the employees, he describes the move towards an overarching green strategy as 'pushing open doors'.

Although it is hard to measure an increase in productivity resulting from a change to an overarching green strategy, the executive director states that '[the employees] are proud of that. Are they motivated by that? I'd say they are, yes. Do they feel better about the organisation? Yes, they do. And does that lead to better performance? It probably does'. Moreover, Interviewee 3 maintains that 90% of the employees state that they are proud to work for their company and that he observes an increase in productivity. However, the same interviewee argues 'I am not saying we are perfect. You always need to ensure that the employees are aligned with the overall strategy and that is why we did this culture change in terms of engaging people into things'. The next section will take a closer look at this cultural change and evaluate the findings on how employee strategic alignment can be reached.

4.3.5 Reaching Employee Strategic Alignment – The Role of Culture

The culture of a company plays a significant role in reaching employee strategic alignment as it builds the link between a strategy and the attitude of employees towards it and enables the rewiring of mindsets. According to all hierarchical levels, a cultural change is imperative to embed the green thinking into employees' daily work. Interviewee 1 states that 'we did a staff survey and it showed that the core cynics have been reduced' after two years of running a cultural change programme. Especially for green strategies, culture plays a significant role as it needs to be understood by all employees that its underlying principles have to be part of the decision-making processes of the company in order to be successful. Hence, Interviewee 2 says that:

> One of the concepts we try to get across is that sustainability is not something different, something extra that you do at your work. It is not really an additional effort. It just takes a bit of a different mindset. So once you've got that mindset [...] you get better efficiency, lower cost, and arguably better well being of the staff.

Interviewee 1 and 2 describe the change of culture as 'a slow moving and multifaceted thing'. They argue that cultural aspects can be found everywhere in a company and are represented by 'routines and rituals around which a company operates'. Interviewee 2 describes these manifestations of culture within the company as 'symbols' and says that 'all of these [symbols] add up to some paradigm of the company'.

Two years after the start of the cultural change programme, the interviewees identify several reasons for the increased strategic alignment amongst the employees. Above all, Interviewee 1 and 2 state that an open culture leads to inspiration and voluntary actions and initiatives that enable alignment and contribute to the successful implementation of a green strategy. Employees require a certain freedom to develop an alignment rather than extra incentives or motivation. Interviewee 1 says that 'the main things that changed have not been money related. It has been when people had the chance to do something inspiring [...] I think the more openness we have and the more people challenge things, the better'. However, the interviewees perceive culture as constantly changing. Even if a culture possesses the above mentioned characteristics to strategically align employees with a green strategy, it needs to be communicated in a way that employees from all hierarchical levels are made aware of the culture they operate in, in order to become committed, contribute, and live it. The executive director describes this progress as follows: 'So two years later, are we changing culture? I think we are. [...] It is a journey, it is not a destination [...] if you would objectively talk to people around the place, I would like to think that they would tell you something similar'. The fact that all interviewees from different hierarchical levels make similar statements suggests that a good communication forms another pillar for the successful change of a culture as well as the strategic alignment of employees.

4.3.6 Reaching Employee Strategic Alignment – The Role of Communication

According to Interviewee 1, communication is 'vital' when it comes to reaching employee strategic alignment with a green strategy. Within the electricity company under study it is used to reduce existing resistance and cynicism among the staff and is especially helpful in changing employees' attitudes towards incorporating green thinking into their mainstream work. Interviewee 2 considers communication as an important cornerstone of strategic alignment and says 'Part of what we try to do is to communicate the strategy. People have to understand it'. In addition to that, the front-line employee points out that especially in a large organisation, it is crucial that the strategy is communicated externally as well as internally in order to reach broad coverage and assure a comprehensive alignment among the employees. He further states that some employees would not even know about the green strategy, but in a company as big as this one he considers it 'normal that some people don't. But every effort is made to also reach those people. And it is done in a good way I'd say'.

The fact that all four employees know and make use of their company's numerous communication possibilities, as well as their awareness of the green strategy and its content proves that the electricity company's communication works and supports the strategic alignment. The interviewees from all hierarchical levels state that the ways their company communicates its green strategy and aligns employees are as manifold as they are transparent. A discussion board on the intranet of the company enables every employee to post comments and debate about the relatively new strategy, which creates an open forum and facilitates a sincere exchange of opinions and views. In addition to that, the organisation uses SharePoint, a monthly internal magazine, e-zines, and a sustainability website to promote their sustainability improvement plans and sustainability charter. This enables everyone within the organisation to get to know the strategy and to compare the achievement of their location with other locations within the country, which in turn facilitates monitoring and reporting and creates healthy competition within the organisation.

Apart from these communication channels the electricity company has set up a green advice bureau, which advises employees how they can act in a more environmental friendly way in their own homes and a road show, which travelled around the country and taught employees about energy efficiency. Recognising the importance of communication and its impact on culture, the organisation introduced green modules into all their company training programmes and created online training modules, which are available to everyone in the company, to align employees to the company's green focus. The organisation realises that in order to communicate a green strategy effectively, all existing communication channels need to mediate a consistent message and additional cross-functional communication is necessary to align employees with their green strategy. Therefore, the executive director encapsulates his company's communication approach as 'relentlessly engaging and communicating and using people to influence other people [to] get people in their hearts to want to do stuff'. Coming from the leader in sustainability, this statement segues from the role of communication to the role of leadership with respect to reaching employee strategic alignment.

4.3.7 Reaching Employee Strategic Alignment – The Role of Leadership

Superiors and their style of leadership within the company under study play a crucial role when trying to align employees with their green strategy. Interviewee 1 considers the commitment of his superiors towards their green strategy as essential and states 'I think we do have the advantage of having a good CEO and that he kind of leads from the top'. He further argues that leadership,

65

engaging employees, and culture are closely linked and that 'It does inspire when [the superiors] are confident behind the strategy and unashamedly putting it out there. Their role is inspiring and good'. The electricity company's awareness of the importance of the leadership role regarding strategic alignment also becomes apparent when Interviewee 2 talks about their road show and says 'And in each location we went, we made sure we brought members of the board of the company and directors into those road shows to talk to the staff about how important this was'. This does not only build up trust in the management and the strategy, but also improves the morale among the employees as an internal survey identifies.

Whether the leadership role is played well or badly and hence leads to successful alignment or not, depends on the authenticity of the leadership style. Interviewee 1 maintains that 'in the green area authenticity is hugely important because there is so much green washing out there [but] the truth comes out sooner or later'. The positive impact of authenticity on employee strategic alignment is also acknowledged by the executive director who says that 'we were going to do everything in here, 7500 of us, we are going to live that kind of dream and [...] make sure that what we were stating as a company externally [are] also delivering internally'. The do-it-yourself attitude of the interviewees shows that the company is true to its word as they e.g. promote and use WebEx meetings to avoid travel and thereby give employees an example of how to live their green strategy.

However, alignment is not only achieved by acting in an authentic manner. The leaders also need to be authentic as well. The positive influence of an honest superior became apparent when the executive director uploaded a webcast to all employees when he was announced to be the new executive director for sustainability. He said that he does not know much about green strategies but is certain that many employees within the organisation do and encouraged them to send him their ideas and promised to involve them. The amount of responses was enormous and indicated the importance of open communication and honest leadership. Despite the findings on the right culture, communication methods, and leadership style the interviews also revealed how additional incentives influence employee strategic alignment which will be further discussed in the following section.

4.3.8 Reaching Employee Strategic Alignment – The Role of Incentives

During all four interviews it becomes apparent that the majority of the employees are highly engaged in their green strategy. Numerous green projects are initiated resulting from ideas of employees which were developed during their free time. The electricity company also started a sustainability champion programme for which employees volunteer to take responsibility for the implementation of green projects and act as a role model for their colleagues. Asking Interviewee 3 if his company provides any extra incentives for encouraging its employees to act in this way or think green he replies with a laugh 'No! It is on top of the day-job', being positively surprised that the employees' approval of the green strategy is so strong. Interviewee 1 concurs with this statement and argues that money would be a wrong incentive to achieve employee alignment with a green strategy. He says:

> I suppose this would be one area where people would be a bit uncomfortable with it, being paid to be more sustainable. [...] I actually find that they aren't motivated by money. I find management has made the mistake ...

assuming that that's the case. And a lot of managements have thrown money at a solution and it actually made things worse. The fundamental motivation that people have ... I've seen it over the 12 years ... people who have been frustrated because they are not getting the fulfilment type of work. They've been promoted maybe or given an extra amount of money but they are the same or even worse.

Resulting from the interviews with the front-line employee and the executive director, it emerges that soft factors such as personal fulfilment rather than money function as incentives to align employees with a green strategy. In accordance with this, the executive director states that the green strategy 'is attractive because it appeals to peoples' values. It actually is aligned with their own values, their own fundamental beliefs and values'. This statement is reflected by the replies and the general demeanour of all interviewees. All of them enjoy being part of a green strategy and are happy to contribute to it. Another indicator for the company's successful employee alignment as a consequence of its cultural change programme in association with the right incentives provides Interviewee 2, who carried out an internal staff survey and states:

> We did one question in the general staff survey last September which was: 'Has your workplace become more sustainable in the last 12 months?' and 'Do you understand what you need to do to work more sustainable?' and the percentage that said 'My workplace has become more sustainable in the last 12 months' was 75%. That is massive. The number of people who said: 'I know what I need to do in my job to be sustainable' was around 70%. [...] We were blown away by that numbers, yeah.

4.4 Research Analysis

To analyse the gathered qualitative data a comparative analysis of the main research findings and the key aspects of the literature is performed. To ensure a reflexive analysis and allow for alternative interpretive perspectives, the chosen categories and sub-categories are compared cross-sectionally by theme (Mason 2002). Furthermore, the comparison of the existing literature with the research findings based on these categories, illustrates that the developed analysis and explanations are tested by trying alternative interpretations and looking for negative instances in particular (Mason 2002).

4.4.1 Implementation of Green Strategies – Differences between Green and General Strategies

Comparing the research findings on the implementation of green strategies with the literature on general strategy implementation, it can be determined that the challenges for both are nearly the same. The statements of the interviewees support the view of Mintzberg (1978) and Nutt (1987) that not only general strategy but also green strategy implementation is not realised in an as straightforward way as planned during its formulation as its process is characterised by 'confrontation and iteration' (Interviewee 2). Additionally, the research findings concur with the theory of Esty and Winston (2009) that every green strategy is unique and its implementation needs to be adapted to the company's specific context. Despite these similarities the biggest difference between the implementation of green and general strategies is that the success of a green strategy implementation depends heavily on the status of the strategy within the organisation. The research findings support the opinion of Esty and Winston (2009) that embedding environmental activities as a
69

core element into an organisation's corporate strategy plays a significant role. Therefore, it can be assessed that the implementation of a green strategy can only be successful if it has an overarching character and at the same time is deeply embedded in the mindsets and attitudes of the employees.

4.4.2 Implementation of Green Strategies – Knowing-Doing Gaps and Performance Paradoxes

According to the findings, the existence of knowing-doing gaps and performance paradoxes as described by Cohen (1998) and Pfeffer and Sutton (1999) is not only a phenomenon related to general strategy implementation, but is also present when putting a green strategy into action. In addition to the existing literature and especially Cohen's (1998) statement that performance paradoxes emerge because people act in contradiction to their instincts or data available to them, the findings add another reason for the occurrence of knowing-doing gaps and performance paradoxes. They point out that some employees are trapped in a daily routine which makes them resistant to change, regardless of the type of newly introduced strategy. The interviewees concur with the techniques proposed by Esty and Winston (2009) to narrow these gaps and tackle these paradoxes for green strategies. Their proposal to set a green agenda with short term, medium term, and long term objectives and reinforce an organisation's vision by stretching its goals is adopted by the electricity company and comes to fruition. Especially the arguments proposed by Kotter (2001), Pfeffer and Sutton (1999), and Semler (2000) to follow a proactive approach by leaders and management to engender a shift in an organisation's philosophy in order to build a framework for an environment with an action related focus are supported by the interviewees. The statements of

Interviewee 2 and 3 that the 'idea of culture change is to make the sustainable way their habitual way' and that 'You need always to ensure that the employees are aligned with the overall strategy' indicate the importance of culture and employee strategic alignment to close knowing-doing gaps and avoid performance paradoxes.

In addition to the predominant conformance, the findings reveal several differences regarding the theory on knowing-doing gaps and performance paradoxes when it comes to the implementation of green strategies. Although Cohen (1998) proposes four conditions which favour the occurrence of performance paradoxes, Interviewee 1 and 4 state that none of them is responsible for the performance paradox within their company. They complement Cohen (1998) by arguing that their middle management is affected by the paradox because their targets do not have a green focus. However, they have to operate between executives and front-line employees who are highly committed and engaged in a green strategy. This leads to a conflict of interest between the middle management and their staff as well as their superiors as the middle management might look at hard targets whereas green goals, which are not included in these targets, are ignored. Despite this additional reason for the occurrence of performance paradoxes, the findings reveal that knowing-doing gaps are indeed present during green strategy implementation, albeit to a lesser extent. The fact that employees identify themselves with the underlying idea of a green strategy, narrows the gap and reduces performance paradoxes as they are automatically more motivated towards the implementation of the green strategy which bridges the role of employee strategic alignment.

4.4.3 Employee Strategic Alignment – Its Role in Green Strategy Implementation

All interviewed hierarchical levels concur with the theory of Boswell (2006) and Noble (1999) that an organisation relies heavily on the commitment and capabilities of their employees when it comes to the organisation's overall performance. By undertaking numerous initiatives such as the transfer of responsibilities for green projects to the employees, the electricity company demonstrates its interest in the alignment of its employees with its green strategy. Doing so, the findings coincide with Gagnon and Michael (2003) and Gottschalg and Zollo (2007), as the company under study aims at a sustainable competitive advantage and an increased competitiveness resulting from the alignment of its employees with its overarching green strategy. Comparing the research findings with the literature, it becomes clear that employee strategic alignment not only plays an important role in green strategy implementation, but that it is the most vital in its success in contrast to the implementation of general strategies. However, despite the significance of employee strategic alignment the interviewees concur with Gottschalg and Zollo's (2007) theory on the unlikelihood of alignment among all employees. Nevertheless, there are several differences regarding employee strategic alignment with green and general strategies which are examined in the following section.

4.4.4 Employee Strategic Alignment – The Differences between Green and General Strategies

One of the biggest distinctions regarding strategic alignment is the predominant willingness among employees to be aligned with a green strategy rather than a general strategy. Although the research findings mainly agree with Gagnon and Michael's

(2003) three stages which have to be passed in order to make strategic alignment possible, a large number of employees do not need to pass these three stages as they are already aligned. Due to the underlying idea of a green strategy, a majority of employees is automatically personally committed and enthusiastic about implementing it. They are proud to work for the greater good and identify themselves with the strategy which leads to happier and personally fulfilled employees and an increase in morale.

This is due to the existing synergy effect between the implementation of a green strategy and employee strategic alignment. Resulting from the conducted in-depth interviews it emerges that an extensive employee strategic alignment does not only lead to a successful implementation of a green strategy, but at the same time the implementation of a green strategy promotes employee strategic alignment. The occurrence of this synergy effect is consistent with the theory of Gottschalg and Zollo (2007) who maintain that two determinants have an influence on the motivation of an employee to behave in a certain way. One is the degree to which the behaviour supports the employee to meet their goals and the second one is the relevance of each goal to the employee.

Furthermore, the findings concur with Noble and Mokwa (1999) who claim that commitment is the cornerstone for a successful strategy implementation. However, the major difference is that for green strategies, this commitment already exists among a certain amount of employees from the start and those who are not committed automatically can be motivated and aligned easier compared to employees working on a general strategy. Despite the concurrence between the interview statements and Gottschalg and Zollo's (2007) theory that there will always be resistant and cynical employees who will not be aligned with any strategy, organisations should be aware of these advantages regarding green strategy implementation. As Interviewee 2 describes it, implementing green strategies is like 'pushing open doors' and organisations would not experience automatic engagement and commitment among their employees with general strategies. Even though a large number of employees is automatically aligned with a green strategy, several other factors can have an impact on the strategic alignment of non-aligned employees and are therefore analysed in the following sections.

4.4.5 Reaching Employee Strategic Alignment – The Role of Culture

Confirming arguments proposed by Esty and Winston (2009) and Pfeffer and Sutton (1999) the research shows that especially for embedding green thinking into an organisation's daily routine culture plays one of the most essential roles. All interviewed hierarchical levels concur with Esty and Winston (2009) that the right culture builds the cornerstone for gaining and maintaining an environmental and sustainable competitive advantage. Research and theory agree that this is due to the ability of a culture to build the link between a strategy and the attitude of employees towards it, as well as to rewire mindsets to reach employee strategic alignment. The research findings additionally support the view of Esty and Winston (2009) that four tools need to be used in order to create a green company culture. The first of these tools, which is a vision reinforced by stretched goals, is especially acknowledged by Interviewee 2 and 4. Secondly, the middle managers as well as the executive director describe the importance of practices that incorporate green thinking into all decision-making processes throughout the organisation. Thirdly, all interviewees address the existing award programmes acting as incentives for committing to and engaging in environmental practices. Moreover, the numerous mentioned methods to communicate their intentions to external and internal audiences are the fourth tool to build a green culture.

Apart from these four tools to create a green culture, the interviewees agree with Pfeffer and Sutton (1999) who argue that a forgiving culture enhances employee strategic alignment. In addition to Pfeffer and Sutton's (1999) statement that a forgiving culture encourages employees to take responsibilities and stimulates them to act, Interviewee 1 and 2 maintain that an open culture leads to inspiration and voluntaristic actions. Hence, research and theory concur that an open and forgiving culture provides the amount of freedom which enables alignment and thereby contributes to the successful implementation of a green strategy. Comparing the research and existing literature on cultural issues, it can be concluded that having the right green culture is vital for the success of a green strategy. However, organisations should keep in mind that culture is a multifaceted and living construct. This is why the executive director for sustainability states that creating a green culture is rather a journey than a destination, and organisations therefore might be able to create the right setting for it but cannot dictate its creation as it needs to evolve.

4.4.6 Reaching Employee Strategic Alignment – The Role of Communication

The research findings indicate that communication is one of the main catalysts of cultural change due to its ability to reduce resistance and cynicism towards a new green strategy and changing employees' mindsets regarding the incorporation of green thinking into their daily routine. In concurrence with Gagnon and Michael's (2003) statement on general strategy alignment, Interviewee 2 maintains that communication plays a crucial role in green strategy alignment as well. Theory and practice agree that its ability to increase knowledge about the strategy around all hierarchical levels serves as facilitator to enhance understanding of the overall goal of the strategy. Supporting Boswell's (2006) view on general strategies, all hierarchical levels agree that employees are also more likely to contribute to a green strategy implementation if they understand their role in it. Additionally, the research findings concur with Noble and Mokwa (1999) and Boswell (2006) that communication is essential to encourage employees to take initiative and thereby create interest in strategy implementation and align them strategically.

Complementing Hambrick and Cannella's (1989) view that internal broad-based selling of the strategy leads to the support of all employees in strategy implementation, the research findings indicate that internal as well as external communication is vital to make a green strategy work and reach employee strategic alignment. The conformity among the statements of the interviewees shows that the communication methods within the company under study work and a consistent message about the green strategy is communicated. Backing up the view of Esty and Winston (2009) that in a transparent world, internal and external communication is a good opportunity to build trust with all stakeholders, the company's numerous communication methods are a good example for how to reach employee strategic alignment. Comparing the literature with the outcomes of the interviews leads to the conclusion that a high amount of internal and external communication methods combined with an attitude to engage employees and appeal to their personal values, increases the chance to align employees with a green strategy. As communication and representing this attitude is mainly the task of superiors, the following section analyses the role of leadership in more detail.

4.4.7 Reaching Employee Strategic Alignment – The Role of Leadership

The evaluation of the existing literature and the research findings illustrates that leadership plays an important role in the success of employee strategic alignment and building a green company culture. Interviewee 2 states that the right leadership style not only builds up trust in the management and the strategy, but also improves the morale among employees which leads to easier alignment. The theory proposed by Pfeffer and Sutton (1999) that this right leadership style is characterised by creating strategy supporting environments, reinforcing norms, and setting expectations through what leaders say and do is supported by the interviewees. By arguing that there is a need for leaders to be and act in compliance with the green strategy, the interviewees agree with Burgelman (1983) and Wooldridge and Floyd (1990) who call this a need for action-managers.

However, the research findings complement the existing literature by pointing out that especially the leadership style within a green environment needs to be authentic. Interviewee 1 states that due to the effect of 'green washing', authenticity is awarded great significance. The findings indicate that honest and authentic superiors who do not only communicate a green message but rather act in an environmentally friendly manner themselves, prove a personal commitment and create an inspiring leadership role for employees. By practising this proactive leadership style, superiors are not only able to create employee strategic alignment with a green strategy, but also create a sustainable competitive advantage (Nadler and Tushman 1990). In addition to the right

77

culture, communication methods, and leadership style incentives are another means to reach employee strategic alignment which will be further examined in the following section.

4.4.8 Reaching Employee Strategic Alignment – The Role of Incentives

The positive effect of incentives on the strategic alignment of employees is neither questioned by the existing literature, nor by the research findings. However, the opinions on the right incentives to align employees with a green strategy diverge immensely. Contrasting with Besser's (1995) view that personal touch money, pay money, and performance related bonuses align employees with the strategy of an organisation, Interviewee 1 argues that money related incentives would be wrong incentives to achieve alignment with a green strategy. Hence, he concurs with Dell and Kramer (2003), who maintain that rather soft factors lead to alignment and thereby to a successful implementation.

The evaluation of the findings indicates that personal fulfilment and value identification are far more important to align employees with a green strategy than money related incentives. Therefore, the findings do not support Gottschalg and Zollo's (2007) view that a combination of extrinsic, hedonic, and normative motivational practices are needed to reach alignment but a combination of hedonic and normative practices is sufficient for an alignment with green strategies. This result concurs with Esty and Winston's (2009) opinion that monetary incentives can be unnecessary and interpreted as unacceptable if green thinking is already embedded in an organisation's mission. Moreover, the comparison of existing literature and research findings illustrates that the proposed award programme by Esty and Winston (2009) is a major incentive and helps to align employees with a green strategy as long as there is no prize money attached to the award. However, the research findings do not only demonstrate that hedonic and normative incentives have a bigger impact on green alignment than extrinsic ones, but also add a new incentive to the existing list. Interviewee 1 argues that acting in alignment with a green strategy is an incentive by itself as it adds experience with green strategies to an employee's skill set and thereby provides a potential career enhancement within companies which have a green focus.

4.5 Conclusion

After analysing the research findings by comparing it to the existing literature it can be concluded that several theories which were developed for general strategies also hold true for green strategies. Two of the most significant conformances are the existence of knowing-doing gaps and performance paradoxes as well as making use of employee strategic alignment to tackle these phenomena for both strategy types. However, the comparison additionally reveals that several theories on general strategies cannot be adapted to green strategies and that green strategies differentiate themselves from general strategies in numerous aspects.

One of the biggest distinctions between the theory on general strategy implementation and the findings is that green strategy implementation can only be successful if the strategy is a core element of the corporate strategy and occupies an overarching character which is deeply embedded in the mindsets and the attitudes of the employees. As the success of a green strategy depends on this overarching character, an open culture and employee strategic alignment are considered even more vital than for general strategies due to their ability to tie in environmental aspects into the corporate strategy and creating the right attitude towards it. Additionally, the findings complement the literature by determining that knowing-doing gaps and performance paradoxes with respect to green strategies exist to a lesser extent and mainly emerge within the middle management rather than among front-line employees. This is due to the fact that green targets are sometimes considered soft and are therefore often not included in management targets or neglected because their performance is measured on hard targets. Furthermore, knowing-doing gaps and performance paradoxes occur to a lesser extent among employees because a majority of employees personally identify themselves with the goal of a green strategy and hence are automatically aligned. Although the findings indicate that employees are generally more willing to be aligned with a green strategy than a general strategy, they agree with the literature on several possibilities to reach strategic alignment among non-aligned employees. Above all, green employee strategic alignment is reached by relentless internal and external communication and authentic action-leadership in combination with hedonic and normative incentives. In addition the findings show that this alignment with a green strategy leads to happier and more personally fulfilled employees and thereby to more commitment. This results in the development of a doing attitude which in turn narrows knowing-doing gaps, reduces performance paradoxes, and leads to a successful implementation of green strategies.

CHAPTER FIVE

CONCLUSION

5.1 Conclusion and Discussion

The green wave and new focus of organisations on environmental friendly business practices demand the opening of a new chapter in literature on theories about successful green strategy implementation techniques. Analysing the existing literature on general strategy implementation and comparing it to the research findings on green strategy implementation, leads to the conclusion that the basic framework for both strategy types may be the same. However, looking under the surface reveals that green strategies need to be approached and managed differently in order to be implemented successfully. While the theory on the occurrence of knowing-doing gaps and performance paradoxes and the importance of employee strategic alignment is applicable to general and green strategies, the extent to which they are applicable differs.

While the theory on general strategy implementation mainly attributes the appearance of knowing-doing gaps and performance paradoxes to front-line employees, the research shows that for green strategies these phenomena emerge less among front-line employees and more within middle management. Apart from the hierarchical shift regarding these phenomena, employee strategic alignment plays a far more significant role for the success of a green strategy than for a general strategy. Due to these two substantial differences, the existing literature on general strategy implementation is only partially applicable to green strategy implementation. However, analysing and evaluating the implementation of green strategies properly can only be achieved by following a separate theoretical approach, merging the suitable existing theory with new insights into successful green strategy implementation.

The fact that aligning all employees from every hierarchical level with a green strategy plays the major role in narrowing knowing-doing gaps and reducing performance paradoxes to facilitate a successful implementation provides organisations with an environmental focus with a huge advantage. Due to the fact that a remarkable amount of employees personally identify themselves with the underlying goal of a green strategy, they are automatically aligned. This leads not only to more action-related behaviour and personal commitment towards the strategy, but also to dedicated employees who create added value by developing and realising green projects in their free time and positively influence their colleagues by promoting green thinking voluntarily. Although this means that knowing-doing gaps and performance paradoxes exist to a lesser extent for green strategies, it does not mean that employee strategic alignment is less important. The opposite is the case. The research shows that a successful implementation is only possible if the green strategy occupies an important part in an organisation's corporate strategy and its overarching character is deeply embedded in the mindsets and attitudes of the employees.

To reach employee strategic alignment and thereby facilitate this overarching character by embedding green thinking in daily work routines as well as all business and decision-making processes, organisations can intervene at several stages. Keeping in mind that greening a business is something to do *with* employees rather than *to* them, organisations cannot force employees to think green, but rather cultivate a green framework by sowing four different seeds which will flourish autonomously. These four seeds, whose reciprocation facilitates reaching employee strategic alignment with a green strategy, are: company culture, communication, leadership style, and incentives.

To close knowing-doing gaps and eliminate performance paradoxes, organisations need to create an open and forgiving company culture which facilitates embedding green thinking into employees' daily routines. By encouraging employees to take responsibilities, providing freedom, and stimulating their attitude towards undertaking green projects, employees feel inspired and an action-based behaviour is developed. The emerging commitment does not only lead to voluntaristic green actions and strategic alignment, but plays a crucial role in gaining and maintaining a sustainable competitive advantage. However, creating the right company culture is closely linked to using the right communication techniques, leadership style, and providing the right incentives. The research confirms that organisations need to communicate their green strategy extensively to all stakeholders, internally and externally. This not only builds trust in an organisations' environmental ventures and catalyses cultural change by reducing resistance against a green course, but increases employees' knowledge and understanding regarding their role within the green strategy. Using discussion boards, monthly magazines, e-zines, improvement plans, training programmes, and online training modules enables organisations to appeal to employees' personal values and thereby encourage employees to take initiative and create interest in green strategy implementation. However, the success of a consistent green message is dependent on the people mediating it, particularly their leadership style. In order to communicate effectively and influence staff and colleagues to act in favour of a green strategy, leaders and superiors need to act as role models. By employing honest and authentic action-managers, who create strategy supporting environments, reinforce norms, and set expectations, organisations are able to create a comprehensive and inspiring leadership style. This proactive leadership improves the morale among employees and hence simplifies the alignment with a green strategy. The right incentives play another essential role in building the right framework for creating a green company culture and closing knowing-doing gaps. Organisations following a green strategy are advised to provide hedonic and normative incentives which aim at soft factors such as personal fulfilment and value identification rather than money. The research identified that money-related incentives do not achieve their purpose if green thinking is already embedded in an organisation's culture. Instead, award programmes for green initiatives lead to alignment and thereby to a successful green strategy implementation.

Many organisations deliberate if going green is the right step into a successful economic future. In addition to the limited resources of the natural world and the growing concern of stakeholders about the environment, this research project identifies another incentive reason to go green. Comparing general to green strategies, more employees are automatically aligned with green strategies as it personally fulfils them to implement a strategy whose values they can identify themselves with. In addition, it is easier to motivate and align employees with green strategies than general strategies. Therefore, organisations which go green face smaller knowing-doing gaps and less performance paradoxes from the outset. Thus, they have fewer difficulties to sell their strategy internally, which results in a more efficient as well as more successful green strategy implementation and lays the foundation for a sustainable competitive advantage.

5.2 Research Limitations

Due to time and resource constraints, the scope and sample size used for this research project is relatively small. Therefore, the findings cannot be generalised to the broader population based on this study alone. Additionally, owing to its qualitative character and the application of in-depth interviews, this research project is subject to criticism regarding the subjective choice of interviewing techniques and interpretations of the research findings. Another limitation to the research is related to the organisation under study. As the electricity company is a semi-state electricity utility, their standpoint and approach towards green strategies might be engendered by different motives compared to other organisations. This also might reflect differently on the behaviour and alignment of their employees. Furthermore, a limitation to the research exists due to the possibility of biased interview partners as they are employed with the electricity company under study and were allocated by the manager for health and environment.

Resulting from these limitations several recommendations for further research emerge. One possibility for further research is to analyse organisations from different industries and compare the findings to the ones presented. Additionally, quantitative research instruments could be used in order to validate the proposed conclusion statistically. Moreover, further research might be able to shed light on change management and its impact of employee strategic alignment and company culture with respect to green strategies. Finally, it would be an interesting avenue to uncover middle managers' perceptions of the identified knowing-doing gaps and performance paradoxes within their hierarchical level in other organisations and compare the outcomes and potential approaches to a solution to the ones presented.

BIBLIOGRAPHY

Argyris, C (1974) Personality vs. Organization. *Organizational Dynamics*, 3(2), 2-17.

Argyris, C (1982) The Executive Mind and Double-Loop Learning. *Organizational Dynamics*, 82(11), 5-22.

Barney, J B (1991) Firm resources and sustained competitive advantage. *Journal of Management*, 17(1), 99-120.

Becker, H S (1993) The epistemology of qualitative research, Working Paper, Paper presented at the MacArthur Foundation Conference on Ethnographic Approaches to the Study of Human Behavior, Oakland, California.

Besser, T L (1995) Rewards And Organizational Goal Achievement: A Case Study Of Toyota Motor Manufacturing In Kentucky. *Journal of Management Studies*, 32(2), 383-99.

Boswell, W (2006) Aligning employees with the organization's strategic objectives: out of 'line of sight', out of mind. *International Journal of Human Resource Management*, 17(9), 1489-11.

Burgelman, R A (1983) Corporate entrepreneurship and strategic management: insights from a process study. *Management Science*, 29(12), 1349-64.

Burrell, G and Morgan, G (1979) *Sociological Paradigms and Organisational Analysis – Elements of the Sociology of Corporate Life*, 1st ed, Ashgate Publishing Ltd, England.

Caldwell, S D, Herold, D M and Fedor, D B (2004) Toward an understanding of the relationship among organizational change, individual differences, and changes in person-environment fit: a cross-level study. *Journal of Applied Psychology*, 89(5), 868-82.

Clough, P and Nutbrown, C (2002) *A Student's Guide to Methodology*, 1st ed, Sage Publications, Inc., London.

Cohen, H B (1998) The performance paradox. *Academy of Management Executive*, 12(3), 30-40.

Colvin, A J S and Boswell, W R (2007) The problem of action and interest alignment: Beyond job requirements and incentive compensation. *Human Resources Management Review*, 17(1), 38-51.

Creswell, J W (1994) *Research Design: Qualitative & Quantitative Approaches*, 1st ed, Sage Publications, Inc., California.

Datamonitor (2009) *Company Profile*, Datamonitor Europe, United Kingdom.

Dell, D and Kramer, R (2003) Forging Strategic Business Alignment, Working Paper, The Conference Board, New York.

Denzin, N K and Lincoln, Y S (1994) *Handbook of Qualitative Research*, 1st ed, Sage Publications, Inc., California.

Denzin, N K and Lincoln, Y S (2000) *Handbook of Qualitative Research*, 2nd ed, Sage Publications, Inc., California.

Dey, I (1993) *Qualitative Data Analysis*, 1st ed, RoutledgeFalmer, London.

Easterby-Smith, M, Thorpe, R and Lowe, A (2002) *Management Research: An Introduction*, 2nd ed, Sage Publications, Inc., London.

Esty, D C and Winston, A S (2009) *Green to gold: how smart companies use environmental strategy to innovate, create value, and build competitive advantage*, rev upd ed, John Wiley & Sons, Inc., New Jersey.

Gagnon, M A and Michael, J H (2003) Employee strategic alignment at a wood manufacturer: An exploratory analysis using lean manufacturing. *Forest Products Journal*, 53(10), 24-9.

Glaser, B G and Strauss, A L (1967) *The Discovery of Grounded Theory*, 1st ed, Aldine Transaction, Chicago.

Gottschalg, O and Zollo, M (2007) Interest Alignment and Competitive Advantage. *Academy of Management Review*, 32(2), 418-37.

Guth, W D and MacMillan, I C (1986) Strategy implementation versus middle management self-interest. *Strategic Management Journal*, 7(4), 313-27.

Halfpenny, P (1979) The analysis of qualitative data. *Sociological Review*, 27(4), 799-27.

Hambrick, D C and Cannella, A A (1989) Strategy Implementation as Substance and Selling. *The Academy of Management Executive*, 3(4), 278-85.

Janis, I L (1982) *Groupthink,* 2nd ed, Houghton Mifflin, Boston, USA.

Harvey, J (1974) The Abilene Paradox: The Management of Agreement. *Organizational Dynamics*, 3(1), 63-80.

House, R J (1971) A Path Goal Theory of Leader Effectiveness. *Administrative Science Quarterly*, 16(3), 321-39.

Hudson, L A and Ozanne, J L (1988) Alternative Ways of Seeking Knowledge in Consumer Research. *Journal of Consumer Research*, 14(4), 508-21.

Hughes, J and Sharrock, W (1997) *The Philosophy of Social Research*, 3rd ed, Pearson Education Limited, England.

Kahn, R and Cannell, C (1957) *The Dynamics of Interviewing*, 1st ed, John Wiley & Sons, Inc., New York.

Kotler, P and Lee, N (2005) *Corporate Social Responsibility – Doing the Most Good for Your Company and Your Cause*, 1st ed, John Wiley & Sons, Inc., New Jersey.

Kotter, J P (1990) What Leaders Really Do. *Harvard Business Review*, 68(3), 103-11.

LaPlante, A (2004) MBA Graduates Want to Work for Caring and Ethical Employers [Online]. Available at:

http://www.gsb.stanford.edu/news/research/hr_mbajobchoice.sht
ml [Accessed 11th June 2010].

Makower, J (2008) *Strategies for the Green Economy: Opportunities and Challenges in the New World of Business*, 1st ed, McGraw-Hill, USA.

Malhotra, N K (2004) *Marketing Research: An Applied Approach*, 4th ed, Pearson Education Limited, England.

Malhotra, N K and Birks, D F (1999) *Marketing Research: An Applied Approach*, 2nd European ed, Pearson Education Limited, England.

Mandelbaum, D G (2008) Seeing Green: Environmental Friendliness as a Business Strategy. *Franchising World*, 40(11), 56-8.

Marcus, A A and Fremeth, A R (2009) Green Management Matters Regardless. *Academy of Management Perspectives*, 23(3), 17-6

Marshall, R and Brown, D (2003) The Strategy of Sustainability: A Systems Perspective on Environmental Initiatives. *California Management Review*, 46(1), 101-26.

Mason, J (2002) *Qualitative Researching*, 2nd ed, Sage Publications, Inc., California.

Miles, M B and Huberman, A M (1994) *Qualitative Data Analysis*, 2nd ed, Sage Publications, Inc., California.

Mintzberg, H (1978) Patterns in Strategy Formation. *Management Science*, 24(9), 934-48.

Mintzberg, H (1987) The Strategy Concept I: Five P's for Strategy. *California Management Review*, 30(1), 11-24.

Mintzberg, H and Waters, J A (1985) Of Strategies, Deliberate and Emergent. *Strategic Management Journal*, 6(3), 257-72.

Morse, J M (1986) *Nursing research methodology: Issues and implementation*, 1st ed, Aspen, Maryland.

Morse, J M (1991) *Qualitative nursing research: A contemporary dialogue*, 1st ed, Sage Publications, Inc., California.

Nadler, D A and Tushman, M L (1990) Beyond the Charismatic Leader: Leadership and Organisational Change. *California Management Review*, 32(2), 77-97.

Nidumolu, R, Prahalad, C K and Rangaswami, M R (2009) Why Sustainability is now the Key Driver of Innovation. *Harvard Business Review*, 87(9), 56-64.

Noble, C H (1999) The eclectic roots of strategy implementation research. *Journal of Business Research*, 45(2), 119-34.

Noble, C H and Mokwa, M P (1999) Implementing Marketing Strategies: Developing and Testing a Managerial Theory. *Journal of Marketing*, 63(4), 57-73.

Nutt, P C (1987) Identifying and appraising how managers install strategy. *Strategic Management Journal*, 8(1), 1-14.

O'Leary, Z (2005) *Researching Real-World Problems: A Guide to Methods of Inquiry*, 1st ed, Sage Publications Ltd., London.

Olson, E G (2008) Creating an enterprise-level "green" strategy. *Journal of Business Strategy*, 29(2), 22-30.

Patton, M Q (1990) *Qualitative evaluation and research methods*, 2nd ed, Sage Publications Ltd., California.

Perrow, C (1993) *Complex Organisations*, 3rd ed, McGraw-Hill, New York.

Pfeffer, J and Sutton, R I (1999) Knowing "What" to Do Is Not Enough: Turning Knowledge into Action. *California Management Review*, 42(1), 83-108.

Placet, M, Anderson, R and Fowler, K (2005) Strategies for Sustainability. *Research Technology Management*, 48(5), 32-41.

Raimond, P (1993) *Management Projects: Design, Research and Presentation*, 1st ed, Chapman & Hall, London.

Rapert, M I, Velliquette, A and Garreston, J A (2002) The strategic implementation process: evoking consensus through communication. *Journal of Business Research*, 55(4), 301-10.

Remenyi, D, Williams, B, Money, A and Swartz, E (1998) *Doing Research in Business and Management – An Introduction to Process and Method*, 1st ed, Sage Publications Ltd., London.

Riel van, B M, Berens, G and Dijkstra, M (2009) Stimulating Strategically Aligned Behaviour Among Employees. *Journal of Management Studies*, 46(7), 1197-26.

Robson, C (2002) *Real World Research*, 2nd ed, Oxford, Blackwell.

Saunders, M, Lewis, P and Thornhill, A (2007) *Research Methods for Business Students*, 4th ed, Pearson Education Limited, England.

Schneider, B, Godfrey, E G, Hayes, S C, Huang, M, Lim, B-C, Nishii, L H, Raver, J L and Ziegert, J C (2003) The Human Side of Strategy: Employee Experience of Strategic Alignment in a Service Organization. *Organizational Dynamics*, 32(2), 122-41.

Semler, R (1994) Why My Former Employees Still Work for Me. *Harvard Business Review*, 72(1), 64-74.

Silverman, D (1998) Qualitative research: meanings or practices?. *Information Systems Journal*, 8(1), 3-20.

Simon, H A (1991) Organizations and Markets. *Journal of Economic Perspectives*, 5(2), 25-44.

Stokes, D and Bergin, R (2006) Methodology or "methodolatry"? An evaluation of focus groups and depth interviews. *Qualitative Market Research: An International Journal*, 9(1), 26-37.

Strauss, A and Corbin, J (1998) *Basics of Qualitative Research*, 2nd ed, Sage Publications Ltd., California.

Sturdivant, J (2008) It's Easy to Be Green. *Wearables Business*, 12(7), 24-5.

Tesch, R (1990) *Qualitative Research: Analysis Types and Software*, 1st ed, RoutledgeFalmer, New York.

Weick, K E and Roberts, K H (1993) Collective Mind in Organizations: Heedful Interrelating on Flight Decks. *Administrative Science Quarterly*, 38(3), 357-81.

Wilson, M (2008) Sustainability Translates into Profitability. *Chain Store Age*, 84(9), 2A.

Wooldridge, B and Floyd, S W (1990) The strategy process, middle management involvement, and organizational performance. *Strategic Management Journal*, 11(3), 231-41.

www.ingramcontent.com/pod-product-compliance
Lightning Source LLC
Chambersburg PA
CBHW071528200326
41519CB00019B/6109